Inquiry
in the
Social Studies
Classroom

A Strategy for Teaching

BARRY K. BEYER
Carnegie-Mellon University

CHARLES E. MERRILL PUBLISHING COMPANY
A Bell & Howell Company
Columbus, Ohio

For Judy

International Standard Book Number: 0-675-09228-0

Library of Congress Catalog Card Number: 76-159110

1 2 3 4 5 6 7 8 9 10—75 74 73 72 71

Printed in the United States of America

Preface

What? Not another book on inquiry?

Right. Another one!

But this one is different.

Much has been written about inquiry and inquiry teaching in recent years. Especially in social studies. Nevertheless, these continue to be subjects of considerable debate—and confusion.

There is a feeling, for example, that "there is less to this inquiry thing than meets the eye." This feeling has grown considerably in recent years with the proliferation of articles and books offering different definitions, models, and descriptions of inquiry, of workshops and panels where theory, argument, and hasty opinion substitute for clarity and practicality, and of the pronouncements of numerous so-called experts who pooh-pooh the whole idea as old hat anyway.

Then, too, there exists the curious paradox best illustrated by those who shrug off inquiry teaching with a curt "Oh that won't work" but almost in the same breath insist "Why, I do that already!" Such an attitude reflects not only the confusion surrounding the nature of inquiry teaching but also the very narrow and foggy perception of what it is in the first place.

There is, in fact, much more to inquiry teaching than meets the eye at first or even second glance. It will work and work well when properly understood and used.

This book is not a plea for the use of inquiry as a teaching strategy. Neither is it an analysis of the merits or deficiencies of inquiry teaching. These have been argued in the literature and at professional meetings for years and presumably will continue to be debated for years to come. Nor does this book discuss whether or not inquiry teaching is "new," for such a discussion would be irrelevant and a waste of time.

Inquiry in the Social Studies Classroom has a different focus. Its sole purpose is to help those interested in using inquiry teaching in their classrooms to come to grips with it so they can devise learning experiences that will truly help students inquire. This book is designed specifically to assist those faced with the daily responsibility of teaching to answer two crucial questions: *"What is inquiry teaching?"* and *"How do I use it in my classroom?"*

These pages are written, of course, out of a deep conviction that inquiry teaching should be the essence of our elementary and secondary school social studies programs today. The reasons for this belief are innumerable. They relate in part to the tremendous explosion of knowledge and rapidity of change that characterize life today. No longer is it possible to teach myriads of facts with any assurance they will be applicable, let alone true, in years to come. No longer can teaching concentrate on passing on almanacs-worth of data. Instead, we must prepare our youth to live satisfying lives in a changing world. And this includes helping them learn how to develop new knowledge from what is already known while at the same time coping with change. This, in sum, means helping them learn on their own, helping them inquire.

It is no secret that school-age children spend more time out of school than in school. A considerable portion of this out-of-school time is still spent in learning, however. And students continue to learn even after graduating—or dropping out. A rewarding, contributing life in a society such as ours requires that our youth know how to use their intellectual abilities rationally. Indeed, the future of our existence as a society may very well depend on this.

Because there is a wide variety of ideas and activities competing for our attention today, it frequently becomes necessary to make choices. For some, choices are made on faith; for others on the basis of some authority. For still others choices are made at a more basic, gut level. None of these ways, however, is sufficient for intelligent social action. A rational way of solving problems is needed.

Moreover, there is today considerable peddling of what others *think* is true as if it were the absolute truth. The clamor to "tell it like it is" seems incessant. News media report an event the way they think it is—or wish it were. So, too, do public figures. And textbooks. And teachers. How many times, for example, have you heard yourself ask: What was the main cause of the Civil War? or What is the major problem facing India today? or Why did Jackson attack the Bank? For each of these questions there is in most classrooms one and only one "right" answer. And the students are queried until they "get it."

Who should decide what is right? Textbooks? Professors? News media? Teachers? Students are usually required—indeed, often willing—to accept without question what so-called authorities say because "They wouldn't go to all that trouble to print it or report it if it weren't true," or because "It's in the book," or because, more practically, those who challenge established authorities usually find that low grades result.

Questions such as those just listed and the belief that anyone can really "tell it like it is" (or was) are naive to say the least. In all frankness we don't know the way it is—or was—or even will be. The best we can do is tell it like we *think* it is. I emphasize the word *think*. Each of us thinks differently. What we think—or know—is, among other things, a product of the questions we ask, our methods of investigation, the quality of the information we use, and our own unique frames of reference. These differ for each one of us.

Apparently we forget that most of what is passed off as knowledge in history and the social sciences is nothing more than interpretation—and someone else's at that. Witness how different scholars examine a major event, such as the Civil War, or major phenomena, such as urban riots or student revolts, and arrive at different conclusions as to their causes. Which interpretation is correct? Which should be taught—and presumably learned—as the truth?

Should it be a function of social studies to stuff children's minds with other peoples' perceptions of reality? To make them first sponges and then parrots? To make their heads nothing more than data storage bins—bins full of answers to questions they never asked? To teach them to accept unquestioningly someone else's perception of "the way it is"—or was? Or should it be a function of social studies to teach youngsters how to establish their own perceptions of reality in more honest, rational, and reliable ways, how to evaluate what others present as the truth, how to find out for themselves?

The answer, it seems to me, is obvious. Our social studies programs must teach children *how to know*—not just what someone else thinks or believes he knows. Students must be taught how to learn on their own through rational inquiry. Suggesting a way to help them do this is precisely what this book is all about.

Of all the different teaching strategies available for the classroom, inquiry teaching appears to be the most reliable method of helping students learn on their own. Experience and research both suggest that students can employ reasoned thinking to give meaning to experience by engaging in inquiry in the classroom. Inquiry teaching is designed to help them do this. Experience and research also suggest that the process of conceptualizing—or developing useful concepts, generalizations, and intellectual skills—may be best facilitated by inquiry teaching.

It is not my intention to describe or elaborate these findings. Dewey, Taba, Massialas, Fenton, Griffin, Metcalf, and others have already addressed themselves to these tasks. This book is not designed to repeat their work. It is designed to carry it one step further.

The pages which follow attempt to describe a practical teaching strategy for using inquiry and to illustrate a variety of ways in which this strategy may be employed in the social studies classroom. My approach is based on a simple proposition—that in order to know how to use inquiry teaching we must first be familiar with what happens when a person inquires. Then and only then can we design learning experiences that will deliberately put students into situations in which they can engage in the various operations which constitute inquiry.

Consequently, this book has three goals: first, to identify the essential elements of intellectual inquiry—of what happens when one attempts to solve a problem or answer a question by the use of reason; second, to describe an instructional strategy (or method) built on this process and designed to foster the use of inquiry in the classroom, a strategy that can serve as a framework both for the conduct of daily lessons and for the construction of units or even courses of study; and third, to analyze some of the implications of the use of this strategy for the teacher, the classroom, and the curriculum builder.

Chapters 1–5 focus on inquiry as a teaching-learning strategy. The nature of inquiry is described in Chapter 1 and illustrated and analyzed through the use of a folktale in Chapter 2. The next two chapters describe in detail a teaching strategy built on this description and also discuss techniques useful in implementing this strategy in the social studies classroom. Chapter 5 attempts to tie together all the preceding points by describing and then discussing an example of an actual inquiry teaching lesson, a lesson in which the reader is encouraged to participate as a learner. Chapters 6, 7, and 8 then discuss in some detail the implications of this inquiry-teaching strategy for concept teaching, curriculum structure, and classroom behavior of teachers and students alike. Finally, a selected list of references and aids is described within a framework designed to help interested teachers gain further insights into the use of inquiry teaching in their classrooms.

There are several notes of caution, however. First, I make no claim to the originality of many of the ideas expressed here. Some of these ideas have been persuasively advanced before by recognized specialists in learning theory and social studies teaching. What is original here, I hope, is how already existing research, discussion, and theory are woven together into a practical teaching strategy—one that can be readily adapted to the realities of daily classroom teaching.

Second, I have not made any attempt to treat inquiry teaching in all its ramifications or applications. I have not, for example, included any extensive discussion of inquiry teaching as it relates to values and value clarification. The reasons for this are threefold. A great deal of interesting writing on this subject already exists (in the work of James Shaver, Donald Oliver,

Louis Raths, Mario Fantini, and Gerald Weinstein, to name just a few). Moreover, most of what is commonly called value analysis and value clarification is not really affective at all. It is cognitive—the learning objective is simply to *know* a particular value or set of values. Hence, what I have written about concept teaching applies equally well to most value teaching. Finally, a number of serious questions need to be raised and explored before we too smugly assume we can—do—or even should—engage in values teaching, clarifying, and analyzing. To explore these questions requires many more pages than are available here and really deserves separate attention elsewhere.

Third, the ideas presented in these pages are by no means to be considered final. On the contrary, they are quite tentative. Most are still evolving. As time goes on many of these ideas will undoubtedly change. Yet, the inquiry strategy described here has already proven itself in classroom instruction for many teachers. It thus appears desirable to share thoughts about this strategy with others interested in inquiry teaching, if for no other purpose than to serve as springboards to improved social studies teaching at all grade levels. It is in this spirit that these pages are written.

A final note before beginning: Reading about inquiry teaching does not automatically enable one to use it with success. To be a successful inquiry teacher requires considerable practice. One must design, teach, and evaluate inquiry lessons and then replan, reteach, and reevaluate them again and again before becoming adept at inquiry teaching. All that can be done here is to present a practical framework for guiding inquiry teaching and to suggest some implications of this strategy for teaching and curriculum development. Becoming familiar with these points is only the first step in introducing inquiry teaching into the classroom. But it is a necessary first step. Once he has taken this step, the teacher can proceed to try inquiry teaching for himself. For, as someone pointed out long ago, we really do learn best by doing!

Carnegie-Mellon University

Barry K. Beyer

Acknowledgments

The ideas expressed here represent the results of considerable study, experimental teaching and reflection, as well as continuous dialogue with social studies classroom teachers, researchers, students, and curriculum developers. I am indebted to these educators for the challenging and stimulating exchange that has generated some of these thoughts.

First and foremost, I wish to acknowledge my indebtedness to six colleagues. I am especially grateful to Professor E. Perry Hicks of the State University of New York at Buffalo for sharing his thoughts and for his suggestions and candid, constructive criticism. Sven E. Hammar, formerly of the Department of History of Carnegie-Mellon University and now of the State University College at Fredonia has made invaluable contributions to this effort, and for these I want to express my most sincere appreciation. Professors Stanley Wronski and Jerry Moore gave invaluable assistance. I am indeed grateful for their thoughtful suggestions. To Ted Fenton and Bertha Davis, who stimulated my interest in inquiring into inquiry in the first place and who provided challenging ideas on which to build, I owe special notes of thanks.

I would like also to express my appreciation to a number of colleagues and former colleagues who have in one way or another contributed significantly to this effort—including Bernie Sauers, Kay Atman, Tony Penna, Jack Mallan, Milt Ploghoft, and Morris Sorin. To the scores of teachers who have listened to my thoughts, questioned them and challenged them, I am most grateful, for without their interest, suggestions, and probing questions the ideas developed here would not have evolved as they did. To all of these people and others too numerous to mention must go considerable credit for whatever makes sense here.

Preparing this manuscript was no easy task. To Ann Hammersla and Rita Pastorelli, whose tireless efforts at the typewriter and the drawing board made it possible to get this to the publisher on time—twice—and to Barbara Hawk, who helped when possible, I wish to express my thanks. The patient comments and timely suggestions of Sue Martin—a tireless editor— have been most helpful in readying the manuscript for publication. Her contributions have been immeasurable. They are deeply appreciated.

Most of all, I wish to acknowledge the support and encouragement of my wife and family. To them go my deepest thanks for their patient under- standing of the long hours required to make this book a reality and for their tolerance of the rather desperate confusion which especially attended the final stages of this effort. They helped make a difficult task a pleasant challenge.

B.K.B.

Contents

The Nature of Inquiry

Inquiry teaching is one of the most exciting types of classroom instruction today. It is the very basis of many of the materials and programs now available for use in various subject areas and grade levels in our schools. It is the essence of the "new" science just as it is of the "new" math. It is basic to some of the newer English and humanities programs and even to the industrial arts. And now, inquiry teaching is offered as the very core of the "new" social studies as well.

What is inquiry teaching? Perhaps the best way to find out is to do it. Let's try.

Among the peoples who live in Africa today are a group who call themselves Asante. *What are they like?*

Most of us may know something about Africans, but we probably don't know much about the Asante. However, if we had a little information about the Asante, perhaps we could answer this question. Here is a list of words commonly spoken by the Asante today. Examine these words and their English meanings. *What are the Asante like?*

Asante	English	Asante	English
abankesee	fort, castle	ɔsom	allegiance
abena	pod	ɔtomfoɔ	blacksmith
adifudee	bargain	bayere	yam
adua	bean	bese	cola
adwa	stool	dwa	market
afiase	shop, store	frafra	compound
afuo	farm	futuro	dust
agrohemmaa	queen	hoahoa ho	boast
agya	uncle, father	kobere	copper
ahennwa	throne	kokoo	cocoa
akotadee	armor	kotoko	porcupine
akuraa	village	kunininana	grandparent
amena	shaft, pit	kwabɔhorɔ	mahogany
ananse	spider	mprampuro	bamboo
apam	alliance	nakumaa	aunt
asafo	company	nana	sir
edɔm	army	nkabɔmu	confederacy
etoɔ	tax	nkoron	mine
obusuani	kinsman	nnɔbaee	harvest
ohuriie	tsetse fly	ntoma	cloth
okra	soul	nwunu	humid
onimdefoɔ	clever	samau	ghost, spirit
onuabaa	sister	sɔsɔ	adze
osidifoɔ	adversary	sika	gold
osuo	rain	siyere	betrothed
ɔhene	chief, king	tɔnkyesem	trickery
ɔhɔhoɔ	alien	teaseenam	car
ɔhokwafoɔ	independent	twene	drum
ɔhyee	heat	wɔfase	nephew
ɔkokobirifoɔ	brave	wesee	dry

List here some of the characteristics of the Asante:

Now, how do you know whether or not these really are characteristics of the Asante? What can you do to find out?

Suppose we had some photographs of the Asante. If the things listed above are really characteristic of the Asante, what do you want to see in these photographs? Pick one or two of the characteristics listed above and then list the evidence you want to see in the photographs that will convince you that what you have listed really are characteristics of the Asante:

On the following pages are four photographs recently taken in Asanteland. Examine them carefully. Can you find the evidence you want to find?

1

2

3

4

What did you find? To what extent did these photos confirm what you thought the Asante were like? To what extent did they contradict your guesses? What characteristics did you list that are neither confirmed nor contradicted by the photos? What new ideas about the Asante do you have as a result of looking at these photos?

Now, *what are the Asante like?*

Finished? At this point you certainly must know something about the Asante—not much perhaps, nor with much certainty, but surely considerably more than when you started. Yet there may be some more questions to answer before you can state for sure what the Asante are like. For example:

> How do you know our list of words are Asante words?
> How do you know these photographs were taken in Asanteland?
> How do you know anything?
> *How do you know?*

Inquiry is one way of knowing. If you became involved in the preceding investigation, if you attempted to work out the answers to the above questions and to any others that may have arisen as you progressed, you were engaging in inquiry. I was engaged in inquiry teaching. These are the subjects of this book.

Inquiry
Teaching

Inquiry is one way of making sense out of what we experience. It requires thinking. And it requires other things, too. Inquiry teaching is putting learners into situations in which they must engage in the intellectual operations that constitute inquiry. It requires learners to make their own meaning out of what they experience. Neither inquiry nor inquiry teaching are easy. But they are productive. And fun!

Inquiry teaching itself is not new. It has been written and talked about for decades. But it has rarely been done. In spite of some attention to it in professional literature, inquiry teaching has seldom been defined clearly enough to be easily mastered. It is still most elusive.

One reason for this is the multiplicity of terms by which inquiry teaching is commonly identified. It is sometimes labeled an approach, sometimes a method, and more frequently a strategy. Terms such as reflective thinking, problem solving, critical thinking, inductive teaching, discovery, and guided discovery are often used to describe it. Obviously, all of these terms do not mean exactly the same thing. Some refer to ways of thinking. Others refer to ways of teaching. Yet they all have one common feature—they refer essentially to a specific way in which people engage in or can be guided in learning. They all are descriptive of something that might best be described as *inquiry*.

But inquiry itself is rather obscure. This is the second reason for the failure to come to grips with this style of teaching. To many people, inquiry is merely asking questions. To others, it is analyzing information, although just what is meant by "analyzing" is not at all precisely defined. To still others, it is synonymous with critical thinking—whatever that is. All in all, there seems to be little agreement about what inquiry really is.

This leads directly to a third reason for a general vagueness about inquiry teaching, that is, a tendency to equate teaching with learning. Experienced teachers know these are not the same, however. Teaching and learning are two entirely different things. Teaching is what teachers do. Learning is what learners do. Unfortunately, there very often is little purposeful relationship between the two.

Yet there should be. Our most effective teaching is built directly on what we know about learning. Unless we understand how children learn, we cannot design experiences that will lead to purposeful learning. This is as true of inquiry teaching as it is of any other style of teaching, for inquiry teaching is based directly on how inquiry as a way of learning is thought to occur.

Teaching— Learning—Knowing

Before exploring how one inquires, however, we ought first to clarify several basic notions about learning and teaching. We need to remind ourselves of the very fundamental relationships that exist between *how* we learn and *what* we learn as well as how teaching is related to both.

Learning and Knowing

Perhaps it is unnecessary to point out here that knowledge and learning are intimately related. No matter. It cannot be repeated too often. *What we know and how well we know it are the products of how we go about learning.* The reverse is also true. *How we go about learning is conditioned by what we know (and want to know) and how well we know it (and want to know it).*

First, let's look at learning. We learn in many ways and for many purposes. Sometimes we learn simply by drill—memorizing. At other times we learn by imitating or copying. Still other times learning is essentially by trial and error. Sometimes we learn by reflecting or thinking about what we see or experience. Each of these ways of learning is different. And so are their products.

For example, sometimes we learn merely by recording what we see, hear, or otherwise experience. We simply etch it on our memory. We don't think about it. We don't take it apart to see how it came to be or how it relates to anything else. We just drill it into our memory. We *memorize* it.

Telephone numbers, street addresses, reigns of kings, and names of capital cities may be learned in this manner. So may concepts and generalizations. Yet, anything memorized is never really known for what it is. Instead it remains a rather superficial bit of information. We may be acquainted with it, but we don't understand it. And we don't know it in the most complex sense of the word "know." Memorizing is not very well suited to building new knowledge—but it is very useful if we wish to learn what someone else thinks is true.

On the other hand when we use what we see, hear, or otherwise experience—when we mentally process it, think about it, reflect upon it, take it apart, and reassemble it in new ways—in order to make sense out of it, we employ a different way of learning. And we learn more than just the information with which we are working. We make this information that we perceive mean something to us. This new meaning becomes our knowledge—what we have learned. We are not just acquainted with it. We understand it. This way of learning is ideally suited for building new knowledge for ourselves.

Second, let's look at a product of learning—knowing. Whatever we know, we know in varying degrees of thoroughness. This is merely another way of saying there are different levels of knowledge. Sometimes we know only in the simple sense of "being aware of." We may, for example, know about the presidency of Abraham Lincoln in the sense that we are aware of the fact that such a person was once president. At another level, knowing may mean a rather superficial "acquaintance with." Knowing of Lincoln's presidency in this sense means knowing a little about this president in relation to other events which can be properly associated with him in a recall situation.

Sometimes, however, we know in a much more complete sense. We understand. We are completely familiar with the major elements of the subject, of their complexities and interrelationships, and of the ramifications of these on each other and on other things properly associated with the subject. This is the highest level of knowing—above simple awareness, beyond superficial acquaintance. Knowing about Lincoln's presidency, in this sense, means a depth of insight into Lincoln's personality, background, actions, and beliefs as well as into the milieu in which he operated as president. Knowing in this sense implies a deep understanding of the *meaning* of whatever is known. This level of knowing is rare, indeed. Yet it is a continued objective of learning.

The thoroughness with which we know something is directly related to how we learn it. Understanding the meaning of something does not result from merely recording and storing. Meaning is not something that can be given intact to anyone. Meaning is made by the learner himself. An individual may become familiar with the fruits of someone else's learning as information, but unless he goes through the mental process of establishing that same learning for himself, he will not really understand it in all its various implications. He may be able later to parrot what someone else thinks is true, but he will lack the insights that constitute true meaning. Meaning—understanding—is built by the learner. It does not exist on its own.

To paraphrase an old adage, we get out of learning exactly what *we put into it*. If we, the learners, put nothing in, if we do nothing with the information with which we are dealing, then all we get is the information that was there initially. But if we work with this information— that is, use it to make it mean something—then we have not only the information used but also its meaning. Developing meaning is the essence of real learning. It requires the learner's deliberate intellectual interaction with information to produce something beyond that information. It is not easy. It requires considerable mental effort. Essentially, meaning making is finding out for oneself. This is the goal, and essence, of inquiry.

Teaching and Learning Strategies

The primary purpose of teaching is to facilitate learning—to stimulate it, guide it, direct it, make it easier, and in general ensure that it happens. How we teach is, or ought to be, related to the kind of learning we wish students to employ and the kind of knowledge we want them to develop. Conversely, whatever kind of learning is used and whatever kind of knowledge is sought prescribe the kind of teaching that ought to be used.

There are many techniques that can facilitate learning: questioning, reading, discussing, copying, role playing, drilling, analyzing, lecturing, reporting, making bulletin boards, writing essays, and so on. The list is practically endless.

Each teaching technique has its own special assets and liabilities. Each may serve a variety of purposes, but none can serve all purposes nor accomplish the job alone. Some techniques are better suited than others for facilitating a certain type of learning. If, for example, we want our students to remember a list of dates or laws or kings or capital cities or other data, the most useful techniques we could employ would undoubtedly include oral drill, recitation, class chanting, copying, or perhaps even quizzing. Teaching in this instance amounts essentially to lesson hearing. The learning that occurs results primarily from memorizing, listening, or repeating.

Because these techniques cannot be used independently of each other, they must be carefully arranged in sequence so as to help the student achieve a learning objective as efficiently and effectively as possible. This is a major task of teaching—to select, arrange, and apply instructional techniques so as to accomplish certain established objectives. Arrangements of teaching techniques are really teaching strategies.

Inquiry teaching is one type of teaching strategy—one way to arrange selected instructional techniques. But only one. There are in reality many different ways to arrange these techniques in order to facilitate learning. Some of these arrangements or strategies are essentially "telling" (expository), while others are primarily "finding-out-for-yourself" (inquiry). As Fenton suggests, these strategies may be represented as the extremes of a continuum on which we can place any type of strategy devised for instructional purposes.[1]

The objective of expository teaching strategies is usually to memorize what someone else says is true. The strategies designed to do this are built directly on learning by memorizing and imitating. Their aim essentially is to supply the student with information which he can later recall. They rely heavily on sources considered to be authoritative—experts, textbooks, traditions, television programs, sound films, and of

---

[1] Edwin Fenton, *The New Social Studies* (New York: Holt, Rinehart & Winston, 1967), p. 33.

course teachers. One such strategy used in expository teaching requires students to:

1. READ

a homework assignment (probably a textbook). Then the students

2. RECITE

in class what has been learned (*recall,* that is, what the reading said) to see if all the essentials have been covered; if not, then the teacher delivers a

3. MONOLOGUE

to clear up any confusion or to add details omitted in the reading. Then, there is a

4. TEST

to see how well the students can recall the material contained in the reading (and the monologue).

This type of strategy is best used to transmit a specific body of knowledge to a student. It requires considerable activity—physical and intellectual—on the part of the teacher, but it does not require much activity on the part of the student. Indeed, while the teacher controls and manipulates the pace, substance, and sequence of what is to be learned, the student remains about as passive as a sponge, absorbing what is poured in and retaining it (hopefully) for regurgitation when triggered by the proper cue on the test that surely will follow. Such a strategy has proven extremely useful in *telling* students all they have to know and in *covering* the text.

Another "telling" strategy, which involves the students to a larger degree, mixes some of the techniques from the preceding strategy with other and alters the sequence. Here the students:

1. READ

a homework assignment (probably a textbook). Then

2. EXPLAIN

to the teacher in class what they read and listen in turn to the teacher explain any corrections or additional information. This latter explanation offers the teacher an opportunity to

3. DEMONSTRATE

what is being considered (perhaps by diagramming
on the board or actually performing a skill so the
students may observe how it is done). Then the students are given an opportunity to

4. APPLY

this by copying the diagram in their notes or using
it to make sense of new data or to practice the skill
by themselves. After this, the teacher may

5. SUMMARIZE

what has been read, explained, demonstrated, applied (and presumably learned) so that a

6. TEST

may be administered to find out how much the students can recall about the topic under consideration.

There certainly is provision for more student involvement in this
strategy than in the preceding one. Some of this involvement is physical;
some is intellectual. Yet the situation still is largely teacher dominated.
He controls the pace, sequence, and substance of what is learned, even
though the student has the opportunity to ask questions and to apply
what he is trying to learn. To the degree that he engages in these activities, the student can become intellectually involved in learning.

Teaching techniques may be arranged in still another way to make
them even more learner centered. The following strategy might be employed by a teacher who wants his class to become more involved in
the learning experience. In this strategy, the learners may:

1. READ

a homework assignment, and then the teacher may

2. EXPLAIN

any aspects that are not clear. The students next

3. RECITE

the basic facts that they have just studied to establish them firmly in their minds and to assure the
teacher that the data has been mastered. The
teacher then may

4. EXPLAIN

additional information that supplements or illustrates the data just presented, and the students then

5. DISCUSS

the implications and possible significance of all this information. Finally, the students

6. SUMMARIZE

in the form of a concluding statement which reasonably accounts for all the disparate details and makes them meaningful.

Even though this strategy is largely expository in its early stages (steps 1–4), the students do build on it; they increase their understanding by manipulating the information they have been given. This requires them to think, reflect, and ask questions. In doing so, they become more intellectually involved than in either of the preceding strategies.

In spite of the presence of some student-oriented techniques in the preceding strategies, all are essentially "telling" strategies. Thus, they are nearer the expository end of the continuum:

E X P O S I T O R Y				I N Q U I R Y
	Read Recite Monologue Test	Read Explain Demonstrate Apply Summarize Test	Read Explain Recite Explain Discuss Summarize	

None of the strategies described here require much more than listening, reading, copying, and memorizing. None are truly learner centered or inquiry oriented, for such a strategy requires the student to use his mind for something other than a data storage bin. Inquiry learning is essentially a way in which the student finds out for himself. Thus, inquiry teaching is a type of strategy that puts the learner into situations which require him to engage in the same operations he would use if he were trying to find out for himself. In inquiry teaching much more than mere listening is required of the student. Indeed, the student must engage in an active intellectual search—a search in which he manipulates data gathered from his or others' experiences or observations or reflections in order to make sense out of it, to give it meaning.

Unlike expository teaching strategies which emphasize the content of the lesson as an end in itself, inquiry teaching requires that learners use this content to develop broader, more meaningful knowledge, skills, or values. Expository teaching appears best suited for covering large amounts of material in short amounts of time. Inquiry strategies are best used, however, for learning beyond the level of simple recognition, for *knowing* in the true sense of the word.

Inquiry teaching is much less teacher dominated or "telling" than is that method of teaching associated with memorizing. Inquiry teaching is much more student centered. Here the student—not the teacher—controls to a greater or lesser degree the pace, sequence, and substance of what is being learned. An inquiry-teaching strategy, simply put, is one that has students identify a problem for resolution, propose possible solutions, test these possible solutions against the evidence, draw conclusions warranted by the testing, and then, later perhaps, apply these conclusions to new data and generalize.

We cannot expect to understand inquiry teaching, however, without some familiarity with the way in which one learns by inquiring. Anyone who wishes to help students learn on their own and learn how to learn on their own must first answer the question: What is inquiry?

The Nature of Inquiry

To many people, inquiry is simply asking questions. It entails much more than that, however. Inquiry is a quest for meaning that requires one to perform certain intellectual operations in order to make experience understandable. Like other ways of learning, inquiry has many components. One of these is, of course, a *process*. But it also is distinguished by a unique set of *attitudes* and *values* as well as by certain kinds of *knowledge*. All three of these, as shown in Figure 1, are part of inquiry.

Knowledge

There are certain things that one must know in order to be a successful inquirer. These include knowing something about the nature of knowledge itself as well as knowing the basic tools of inquiry, their functions, and how to use them.

1. About the nature of knowledge. What we know, as individuals or groups, is never complete or final—it is constantly changing and

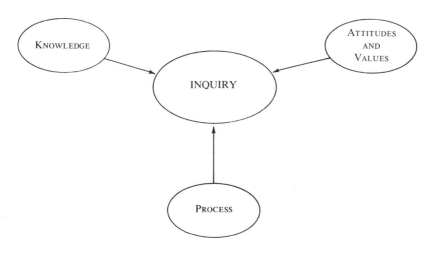

FIGURE 1

therefore quite tentative. Moreover, what passes for knowledge is actually nothing more than interpretation. In order to learn by inquiring, one must understand these three points, know why they are so, and understand their implications for trying to determine the "truth" about anything.

The amount of information and knowledge we are accumulating today doubles about every ten years. As it does, suspected truths may be substantiated, whereas accepted truths may be questioned, challenged, or proved invalid. To the inquirer, recognition of this fact means that what we accept as true today is only tentative and therefore subject to change in the light of future information and investigation.

Moreover, knowledge is at best fragmentary. It is rarely complete. We cannot secure absolutely all the information necessary for making a judgment that will stand forever. This is due partly to the difficulties of locating and collecting all pertinent information and also to the fact that since knowledge is a product of the human mind, it is subject to all the peculiarities of that mind at work.

In the last analysis, what passes for knowledge is really only interpretation. It is the product of minds dealing with reality in terms of their own past experiences. Each individual lives an experience that is unique to him and, as a result, develops a special set of prejudices, biases, likes, dislikes, inclinations, and ideas. All of these together comprise a frame of reference which shapes the way he perceives and reports reality. This frame of reference conditions what we select to perceive, the questions we ask of experience, how we deal with what we notice, and how we report it. Consequently, what we report as the truth—the end product of some perception of reality—is not the way it really is but merely the way we think it is, the way we perceive it to be. It is not absolute truth—it is only our approximation of it.

A good inquirer knows that what is touted as knowledge—as fact—is only someone's opinion of reality and that that opinion is colored by a frame of reference or background of experience unique to that individual. This means that different people can have very similar experiences or work with the same data and legitimately arrive at different —but equally reasonable—answers. There can be many sides to the same question. An inquirer knows that it is important thus to investigate all of these sides, to be aware of how a frame of reference shapes "knowledge," and to make every effort to identify these sides in dealing with what others report as knowledge.

There are other implications, too. Knowing that knowledge can be determined in a variety of ways—by word of some authority, by superstition, and by very superficial examination of the data, for instance—means that what is reported as true may or may not be a fairly accurate representation of reality. This means, in sum, that the accuracy of what is known, the degree to which it corresponds with reality, is determined ultimately by the quality and quantity of the relevant evidence and by the way in which it is manipulated—that the closest approximation to the way things really are or were can only come through honest and sustained intellectual inquiry.

Of course, it is important to recognize that some experts have spent most of their lives researching in their respective fields and may be closer to reality in those fields than some novices are ever likely to be. Thus, in the search for knowledge it is not always necessary to go through the process of original investigation. Instead, we may examine the qualifications of the experts who are already at work, and we might also examine the quality of their work. What they have learned may become information for us to use in our learning. Or flaws discovered in their work may reveal a need for further research. A good inquirer realizes these facts, too.

2. *About the tools of inquiry.*   In order to inquire productively, one must also understand the nature and function of the tools of inquiry. These tools include certain types of sources of information, basic concepts which can help analyze experience, and a process of rational inquiry itself.

Inquiry requires a knowledge of where to find reliable, up-to-date *sources* of primary information, reports by others of what they believe to be true, and accounts of events or experiences or other useful information. Inquiry also demands an understanding of the strengths and weaknesses of each of these as reliable and valid reports of reality and a knowledge of how to work with them to compensate for any distortions or inaccuracies. It means knowing how to use a library, read a newspaper, listen to a speech, evaluate a personal experience, and so on.

Concepts are also important tools of inquiry. Concepts give rise to questions which may be asked of experience or data to make it meaningful. In addition, they serve to organize disparate information into categories and patterns which reveal meaningful relationships. Concepts not only represent knowledge, they help to produce knowledge.

Although there are an almost infinite number of concepts one might know or use, some are more useful to inquiry than others. These concepts are the ones that generate useful questions to ask of experience—analytical concepts, as Fenton calls them.[2] Such concepts might include areal association, status, leadership, and scarcity, for example, each of which may be applied to the analysis or structuring of a wide variety of data. They may be used to sift through this data in order to make it meaningful.

Concepts are extremely important to successful inquiry—so much so, in fact, that they deserve separate treatment at a more appropriate place (see Chapter 6). It should be sufficient to note at this point that they are the most basic tools of intellectual inquiry. Knowledge of them is absolutely essential to productive inquiry teaching and learning.

Another basic tool of inquiry is a *process of rational investigation.* In order to be successful at inquiring, one must understand this process, know how it works, the interrelationships of its different operations, and the implications it has for learning and knowing.

There are, in sum, certain kinds of knowledge essential to successful inquiry (see Figure 2). They are quite different from what other learning methods demand.

Attitudes and Values

Just as one must have certain kinds of knowledge, so too must he possess certain attitudes and values if he is to be a successful inquirer. In most instances these attitudes and values are derived from or at least associated with the kinds of knowledge just described. Moreover,

---

2 Edwin Fenton et al., *A High School Social Studies Curriculum for Able Students: Final Report of USOE Project HS-041* (Pittsburgh: Social Studies Curriculum Center, Carnegie-Mellon University, 1969), pp. 25–27.

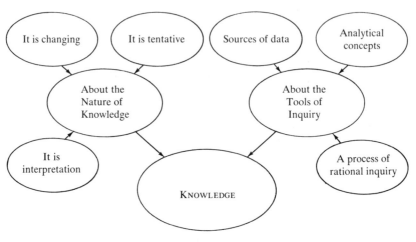

FIGURE 2

they are not generally characteristic of other ways of learning. A successful inquirer, for example, must value objectivity and the use of reason to solve problems. He must respect evidence as the test for accuracy. He must be willing to suspend judgment and, to a point, be tolerant of ambiguity. Above all, he must be curious and imaginative. Each of these attitudes and values plays an important part in inquiry either by making it possible or by sustaining it.

1. Skepticism. The keystone of inquiry is skepticism, a kind of questioning attitude that doubts simplistic answers or single-factor causes and solutions. It is generally reflected in a reluctance to accept old interpretations or the assertions of so-called authorities as the final truth and, conversely, in a desire to find out for oneself. It is a doubting feeling that leads to a reluctance to accept things as they are reported by others and to a willingness to suspend judgment while the search for truth goes on. It not only helps generate inquiry but also stimulates and guides it.

2. Curiosity. Skepticism implies curiosity, for even though one doubts something, inquiry will not take place unless he is curious enough to want to know more or better about it. Curiosity is an attitude of wanting to know. It is closely related to and derived from imagination—that realm of fanciful thinking that enables one to go beyond the way things appear to postulate possible solutions to problems, create hypothetical alternatives, or invent new ways of viewing or dealing with tasks. Curiosity, imagination, and skepticism generate and sustain inquiry.

3. Respect for the use of reason.   One is not likely to inquire unless he values the use of rational investigation as the best way to learn. Given a choice between relying on an authority's answer to a fundamental question or problem (such as, "Why did the United States get involved in Vietnam?" or "Is one race inferior to another?" or "What is my proper relationship to my government?") or finding out on his own by inquiry, he will select the latter. Of course, he will readily consult reliable sources of specific information, for he would be foolish not to take advantage of the valid inquiry of others. But on problems of major import he will use these sources to find out for himself rather than memorize them unthinkingly.

4. Respect for evidence as a test for accuracy.   There are many tests for truth. One which is essential to inquiry is the quality and quantity of the evidence relative to the question, problem, or task at hand. The successful inquirer is one who values this evidence as the final determinant of the accuracy of opinions or hypotheses—not the assertions of some textbook, television speaker, teacher, or next-door neighbor.

5. Objectivity.   Because an inquirer knows that what people report as true is really only a perception of what they think is true, because people perceive things differently due to their own special frames of reference, he knows that there are several sides to every question. Consequently, he realizes the need to search out and examine all possibilities in a way as dispassionate and unbiased as possible. This means that the inquirer must deliberately search for evidence contrary to what he expects or wants to find and must evaluate it fairly rather than hastily dismiss it as worthless. He must be aware of his own biases and prejudices and strive to avoid allowing them to distort the data with which he works or the ways in which he works with it. Even though he may very well be subjective about the kind of questions he chooses to ask, he must be as objective as possible in how he inquires.

6. Willingness to suspend judgment.   This is very closely related to a respect for objectivity and grows out of the same knowledge. A willingness to suspend judgment involves the realization that it takes time to locate sufficient evidence to prove a point beyond a reasonable doubt. Although one cannot wait to make a decision or judgment until all the evidence has been accumulated—because it rarely, if ever, is possible to secure all the relevant data on any point of inquiry—one must still hesitate to jump to conclusions before sufficient data has been examined. To examine one or two major wars and then conclude that all wars are caused for economic reasons would certainly be inappropriate and invalid. Instead, a larger number of wars—more data—must be analyzed before a judgment may be pronounced with any degree of credibility. This requires that the inquirer be most hesitant to jump to final conclusions.

7. *Tolerance for ambiguity.*   A desire for certainty is a human characteristic. People have varying degrees of tolerance for uncertain, ambiguous, open-ended situations. Some can stand considerable ambiguity without any adverse reaction, while others can stand very little. This tolerance and intolerance for ambiguity play a key role in inquiry.

The degree to which one can tolerate uncertainty may be viewed as a continuum running from a high degree of tolerance on one end to almost intolerance at the other.

Many people have a certain amount of tolerance for ambiguity; open-ended or unsettled situations do not bother them. This makes possible the acceptance of what appears to be an answer even though all the evidence may not yet be in. Sometimes it even makes people willing to accept the unsettled nature of a task, to tolerate the absence of an answer, and in no way to desire closure. The uncertainty is so minor that it just doesn't bother them at all.

At a certain point, however, a point which varies according to the individual, an end to ambiguity is sought. People want certainty. At this point they want an answer, and they will move actively to seek it. A growing intolerance for any more ambiguity motivates them to seek a solution, to tie up loose ends, to draw some degree of certainty out of uncertainty. It is this pursuit that leads to learning and sustains inquiry— the learner's desire for an answer, not to satisfy the teacher but to satisfy himself.

Yet there is another point on this continuum beyond which inquiry is inhibited. At this point one can no longer tolerate any more ambiguity, and his frustration turns him away from the effort of learning or inquiring. He divorces himself completely from the learning situation.

Understanding this attitude toward ambiguity is basic to inquiry because inquiry is actually built on the natural human desire to close the gap between uncertainty and certainty. There must be some degree of ambiguity or inquiry does not occur. On the other hand, there cannot be too much ambiguity or people will just turn away from it. A willingness to tolerate uncertainty to a point is useful in motivating inquiry and in dealing with a lack of essential data. A good inquirer has a low "turn-on" point and a high "turn-off" point.

All of these values and attitudes comprise an integral dimension of inquiry. Together they motivate and guide the way in which one inquires.

They grow, in general, out of what one knows about knowledge and the tools of inquiry and life itself. They may be summarized by the diagram in Figure 3.

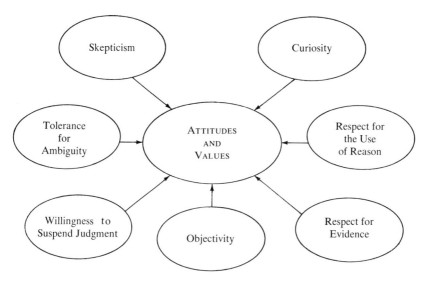

FIGURE 3

A Process

Inquiry demands not only the knowledge of how to inquire and the possession of attitudes and values supportive of this way of learning, but it also requires working with data or experience in a special way. This way can best be described as process.

The process of inquiring grows out of the attitudes, values, and knowledge already described. It is sustained and guided by them. It is intellectual in nature, for it is essentially a mental operation. It is not just a single act but rather a complicated series of related acts, each of which consists of a number of unique intellectual operations. It requires an individual first to define a purpose for inquiring and then to guess at a tentative answer or solution—to hypothesize. Thereafter, he must test his hypothesis against relevant data and finally draw a conclusion about the validity of his hypothesis.

1. Defining a purpose for inquiring. Inquiry commences when one feels a need to know something. This "something" may be an answer to a question or problem, a bit of information needed to satisfy a curiosity, or some information that is sought to bring closure to an otherwise unsettled experience. The first major step in the process of inquiring is to make the task explicit, to define it in manageable terms, and to set the limits of the quest. One cannot inquire successfully unless he has a fairly accurate idea of what he is looking for or what he needs to know.

2. *Guessing at a tentative answer or solution—hypothesizing.* A hypothesis is a tentative answer to a problem or question. Once a purpose for inquiry has been delimited—such as, "What causes war?"—one can make a guess as to the possible answer—perhaps, in this case, "War is caused by greed." This guess is based on the available data plus the background of experience of the inquirer and is conditioned by his own particular frame of reference. Such a guess then determines the nature of the ensuing inquiry.

3. *Testing the hypothesis.* After a hypothesis has been formulated, it must be tested to see how well it is supported by the relevant information. This operation is often long and involved, for it includes gathering data, evaluating it, and analyzing it in terms of the hypothesis being tested. Even the process described as "analysis" is quite complicated; it involves intensive examination of the data to see to what extent it supports or refutes the hypothesis.

4. *Drawing a conclusion.* Inquiry culminates with a decision about the validity of the hypothesized answer to the initial problem or question. In this stage of the process, the inquirer determines to what degree the evidence he has analyzed makes his hypothesis valid or invalid. If the evidence supports his guess, then he accepts it as a much more definite answer or explanation. If the evidence does not support the hypothesis, however, he must retrace his steps, hypothesize a second explanation, and proceed to test that. Drawing a conclusion about the validity of a hypothesis is often a culminating if not always final step in inquiring.

5. *Applying the conclusion to new data and generalizing.* The quest for meaning usually leads an inquirer beyond a simple conclusion, however. In the course of his experience he has repeated opportunities to test his conclusions against new but related experience or data. He treats his conclusions as hypotheses to see if they stand up in the face of the new data. As he does this, he also broadens his conclusions to explain this new data. Sometimes in so doing the original conclusion is modified or altered. Certainly it becomes more general and less tied to specifics. Concepts emerge in this way. So do generalizations—broad statements about the relationships between several classes of data or between several concepts. Regardless of what the ultimate general statement is labeled,

however, this operation represents the final step in the process of making experience meaningful.

These five operations comprise the main steps in the process of inquiring. They are sequential in that defining a purpose for inquiry must precede the other steps, hypothesizing can only occur after a problem has been identified but must occur before meaningful analysis can be undertaken, and so on. This process may be visualized as in Figure 4.

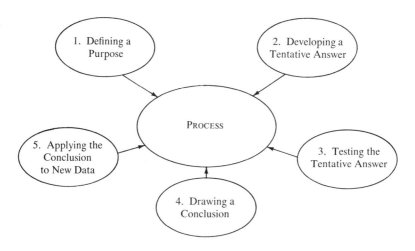

FIGURE 4

The process of inquiring is one way of making sense out of what we see or hear or read or otherwise experience. It is one way of making things mean something to us. The operation of this process is obviously much more complex than outlined here. But this description will do for a start. It should be sufficient to remember at this point that the process of inquiring is the key to inquiry. It is this process of determining meaning that makes inquiry as a way of learning different from other ways of learning.

Inquiry itself is more than a process, however. It has three major dimensions: a certain number of attitudes and values, certain knowledge, and a specific process. Although these dimensions have been separated from one another here for purposes of analysis, they are in practice inseparable. No one part operates completely independently of the others. Inquiry is, indeed, a very complex way of learning. It may be visualized as in Figure 5.

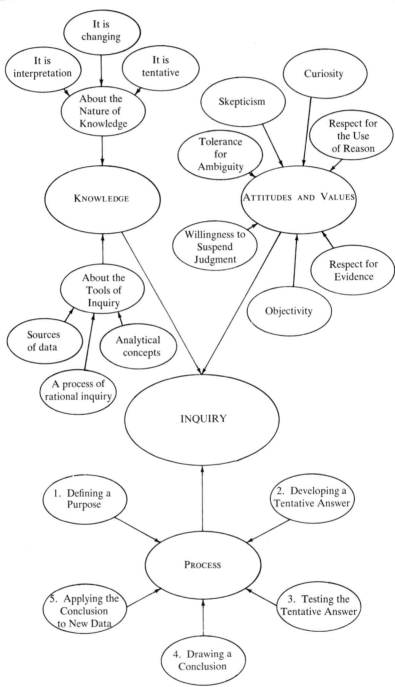

FIGURE 5.   A Concept of Inquiry

There undoubtedly are a number of ways to conceptualize inquiry. But whatever way is used, it should include at least the three dimensions described here. For inquiry is more than process, and until this is clearly understood, the development and use of practical teaching strategies based on inquiry will be nearly impossible.

The Process of Inquiring

2

Inquiry is more than an abstract concept. It is a very real type of behavior. As long as it is dealt with only in abstract terms, it is likely to remain vague and elusive if not actually confusing. To make it more concrete, to understand it better, we ought to use this concept to analyze samples of behavior that purport to be inquiry in nature. In doing this the very skeletal outline described in the preceding chapter may be fleshed out and made considerably more substantial. It is the purpose of this chapter to help do just that.

It Was Obvious

Professional education literature abounds with many examples of inquiry in action. Most of these are transcripts of actual classroom dialogues. The example that follows here, however, is different. It is a brief folktale—fiction, of course—about a scholar who is an expert Jewish theologian. Marmaresch, the community referred to, was a typical shtetel, an area inhabited by Jewish people in the late nineteenth-early twentieth centuries in southeastern Europe. Because the scholar is native to southeastern Europe, he is well acquainted with its inhabitants and quite familiar with the people of the surrounding areas. Thus he is able to make the assumptions he does.

This particular tale is a translation from a collection of folk humor originally published in 1947. It is worth reading twice. First, read it as a story. Attention should be given to the literal meaning only. Nothing need be read into it, for it is not the content that is of major concern. The main interest here is the process used by the scholar to solve his problem. Then the tale should be read a second time for evidence of the basic elements of inquiry as represented in Figure 5. To what extent is inquiry evident in this tale?

> A Talmudic Scholar from Marmaresch was on his way home from a visit to Budapest. Opposite him in the railway carriage sat another Jew, dressed in modern fashion and smoking a cigar. When the conductor came around to collect the tickets the scholar noticed that his neighbor opposite was also on his way to Marmaresch.
>
> This seemed very odd to him.
>
> "Who can it be, and why is he going to Marmaresch?" he wondered.
>
> As it would not be polite to ask outright he tried to figure it out for himself. "Now let me see," he mused. "He is a modern Jew, well dressed, and he smokes a cigar. Whom could a man of this type be visiting in Marmaresch? Possibly he's on his way to our town doctor's wedding. But no, that can't be! That's two weeks off. Certainly this kind of man wouldn't twiddle his thumbs in our town for two weeks!
>
> "Why then is he on his way to Marmaresch? Perhaps he's courting a woman there. But who could it be? Now let me see. Moses Gold-man's daughter Esther? Yes definitely, it's she and nobody else . . . ! But now that I think of it—that couldn't be! She's too old—he wouldn't have her, under any circumstances! Maybe it's Haikeh Wasservogel? Phooey! She's so ugly! Who then? Could it be Leah, the money-lender's daugher? N—no! What a match for such a nice man! Who then? There aren't any more marriageable girls in Marmaresch. That's settled then, he's not going courting.
>
> "What then brings him?
>
> "Wait, I've got it! It's about Mottell Kohn's bankruptcy case! But what connection can he have with that? Could it be that he is one of his creditors? Hardly! Just look at him sitting there so calmly, read-ing his newspaper and smiling to himself. Anybody can see nothing worries him! No, he's not a creditor. But I'll bet he has something to do with the bankruptcy! Now what could it be?
>
> "Wait a minute, I think I've got it. Mottell Kohn must have cor-responded with a lawyer from Budapest about his bankruptcy. But that swindler Mottell certainly wouldn't confide his business secrets

to a stranger! So it stands to reason that the lawyer must be a member of the family.

"Now who could it be? Could it be his sister Shprinzah's son? No, that's impossible. She got married twenty-six years ago—I remember it very well because the wedding took place in the green synagogue. And this man here looks at least thirty-five.

"A funny thing! Who could it be, after all . . . ? Wait a minute! It's as clear as day! This is his nephew, his brother Hayyim's son, because Hayyim Kohn got married thirty-seven years and two months ago in the stone synagogue near the market place. Yes, that's who he is!

"In a nutshell—he is Lawyer Kohn from Budapest. But a lawyer from Budapest surely must have the title 'Doctor'! So, he is Doctor Kohn from Budapest, no? But wait a minute! A lawyer from Budapest who calls himself 'Doctor' won't call himself 'Kohn'! Anybody knows that. It's certain that he has changed his name into Hungarian. Now, what kind of a name could he have made out of Kohn? Kovacs! Yes, that's it—Kovacs! In short, this is Doctor Kovacs from Budapest!"

Eager to start a conversation the scholar turned to his travelling companion and asked, "Doctor Kovacs, do you mind if I open the window?"

"Not at all," answered the other. "But tell me, how do you know that I am Doctor Kovacs?"

"It was obvious," replied the scholar.[3]

What elements of inquiry can be identified in this story? Here is a man who finds himself in a problematic situation. He could solve his problem by asking his traveling companion his name. But he does not. Instead, he proceeds to think out the answer for himself, to reflect, to inquire. He obviously values the use of this method as a way to solve problems and to learn.

There is evidence of other inquiry attitudes here. This scholar is certainly curious! A situation that undoubtedly is not at all problematic to many people on this train bothers him. One reason for his curiosity is the proximity of the problem to him. It is close, relevant. Another reason is that what he perceives does not make sense. He is a keen observer and has a wide background of experience. He also has a low tolerance for ambiguity—thus he wants to know "Who can it be, and why is he going to Marmaresch?" And he does not give up easily in his

[3] Reprinted by permission of Schocken Books Inc. from *Röyte Pomerantsen,* edited by Immanuel Olsvanger, copyright © 1947 by Schocken Books Inc. Translation taken from *A Treasury of Jewish Folklore* by Nathan Ausubel. © 1948 by Crown Publishers, Inc., pp. 7–8. Used by permission.

quest for an acceptable answer. In spite of several dead ends, he pursues the evidence until he arrives at a conclusion that proves valid, at least to his satisfaction. He is willing to suspend a final judgment until all relevant evidence is in; he examines as many sides of the problem as possible; and, finally, he has a healthy respect for evidence—he uses a considerable amount in the process of testing his guesses as to the identity of his traveling companion.

This scholar obviously knows how to inquire. Perhaps that is what makes him a scholar. At any rate, he has command—knowledge—of the basic tools of inquiry: sources of data, analytical concepts, and a process of inquiring itself. Interestingly enough, his prime data source is his memory. Over the past years he has stored away, just as all people do, bits and pieces of information and experience that he now finds relevant to the problem at hand. He also secures a considerable amount of data by observing his subject. In addition, he has certain concepts—of courtship, of bankruptcy, of Budapest lawyers—that lead him to ask certain questions whose answers guide his analysis of all relevant data. There can be little doubt as to his familiarity with rational inquiry.

If it is nothing else, this story is vividly descriptive of inquiry in action. After sensing a problem that almost demands a solution, our scholar proceeds to hypothesize and then to test his hypotheses until he comes up with a solution to the problem. What happens as he does these things?

Defining the Problem

Our scholar is apparently en route to the town of Marmaresch. He boards a train, perhaps in Budapest, and seats himself with other passengers in one of the coaches. Suddenly he becomes aware of a situation which puzzles him:

> . . . Opposite him in the railway carriage sat another Jew, dressed in modern fashion and smoking a cigar. When the conductor came around to collect the tickets the scholar noticed that his neighbor opposite was also on his way to Marmaresch.
>
> This seemed very odd to him. . . .

Certainly such a well-dressed man has no business going to Marmaresch, or so our scholar thinks. He evidently knows enough about this little town to realize that some special occasion must be calling this gentleman to visit there. He is curious—"Who can it be, and why is he going to Marmaresch?" His statement of the problem is simple and direct. He is starting to inquire.

Our scholar doesn't jump to any hasty conclusions. Nor does he tackle the whole problem all at once. Instead, he breaks it into a number of sub-problems, the answers to which gradually lead him to a valid resolution of the main problem. He elects first to figure out why this man is going to Marmaresch, thinking perhaps that if he can determine this, he will have some clues as to who the man is. So his immediate problem is ". . . why is he going to Marmaresch?"

Hypothesizing and Testing the Hypotheses

Our scholar studies the subject of his curiosity and notices that he is well dressed, modern, and apparently reasonably wealthy. He then attempts to recall information about the town that might suggest why a man like this is traveling there. As he does, he suddenly comes up with a possible reason—the town doctor's wedding. However, examination of further information about the date of the wedding and the apparently sleepy, dull nature of the community itself suggests that this hypothesis is unacceptable. So he rejects this as the answer and returns to the problem once again.

"Why then is he on his way to Marmaresch?" Courtship! A second hypothesis. So he dredges up some more information relevant to this guess:

> ". . . Moses Goldman's daughter Ester? Yes, definitely, it's she and nobody else . . . ! But now that I think of it—that couldn't be! She's too old—he wouldn't have her, under any circumstances! Maybe it's Haikeh Wasservogel? Phooey! She's so ugly! Who then? Could it be Leah, the money-lender's daughter? N—no! What a match for such a nice man! Who then? There aren't any more marriageable girls. . . ."

Again, analysis of the evidence fails to yield anything that leads him to believe this gentleman could be courting a girl from the town, so he concludes that this hypothesis is inaccurate. Thus, he discards it, too.

"What then brings him?" Our scholar returns to the original problem. Suddenly he recalls some more information about events in the town which appears to offer a reasonable answer. Bankruptcy! This is his third hypothesis:

> "Wait, I've got it! It's about Mottell Kohn's bankruptcy case!"

Concluding

At this point the inquiry into the initial sub-problem comes to a close. Our scholar does not discard the idea of bankruptcy but accepts it as the reason for this man's going to Marmaresch. He does so simply because all other reasonable explanations have been eliminated. As the last remaining apparently logical explanation, this reason merits consider-

ation. For him, at least, part of the original problem is now solved—even
if only tentatively.

Defining the Problem

The main problem still remains, however. "Who can it be . . .?" Having
decided why the stranger is on his way to Marmaresch, our scholar
assumes then that this man must have some connection with the bankruptcy. Determining this connection will help determine his identity. So
he asks himself, ". . . what connection can he have with that?" A new
problem!

Hypothesizing and Testing the Hypotheses

Once again he guesses at an answer:

> "Could it be that he is one of his creditors? Hardly! Just look
> at him sitting there so calmly, reading his newspaper and smiling
> to himself. Anybody can see nothing worries him! No, he's not a
> creditor. . . ."

So that hypothesis is discarded and a new line of inquiry posited. What
other kinds of people are usually involved in bankruptcy cases? Lawyers.

> ". . . Wait a minute, I think I've got it. Mottell Kohn must have cor-
> responded with a lawyer from Budapest about his bankruptcy. . . ."

Concluding

This makes sense! Now our scholar thinks he is on the right track. His
traveling companion must be a lawyer. He is one step closer to answering
his original question "Who can it be . . . ?"

Problem-Hypothesis-Test-Conclusion

He now turns to another sub-problem. Since he knows Mottell Kohn
quite well, or at least thinks he knows him, the solution appears to be
relatively easy:

> "But that swindler Mottell certainly wouldn't confide his business
> secrets to a stranger! So it stands to reason that the lawyer must
> be a member of the family. . . ."

All he needs to do now is figure out which relative it could be. An answer
is not long in coming. First he states the problem again. Then he hypothesizes. His initial hypothesis is rejected because it is not supported
by the available data—the date of the marriage and the apparent age of
the man in question. But then, suddenly, everything seems to fall into
place:

"Now who could it be? Could it be his sister Shprinzah's son? No, that's impossible. She got married twenty-six years ago—I remember it very well because the wedding took place in the green synagogue. And this man here looks at least thirty-five.

"A funny thing! Who could it be, after all . . . ? Wait a minute! It's as clear as day! This is his nephew, his brother Hayyim's son, because Hayyim Kohn got married thirty-seven years and two months ago in the stone synagogue near the market place. Yes, that's who he is!

"In a nutshell—he is Lawyer Kohn from Budapest. . . ."

Yet, even though he knows or thinks he knows who the man is, there are several other minor problems to be dealt with:

"But a lawyer from Budapest surely must have the title 'Doctor'! So, he is Doctor Kohn from Budapest, no? But wait a minute! A lawyer from Budapest who calls himself 'Doctor' won't call himself 'Kohn'! Anybody knows that. It's certain that he has changed his name into Hungarian. Now, what kind of a name could he have made out of Kohn? Kovacs! Yes, that's it—Kovacs! In short, this is Doctor Kovacs from Budapest!"

Finally, a conclusion, an answer to the whole problem "Who can it be . . . ?" Our scholar has gone as far as he can go on his own. But because he is human and because he too cannot tolerate too much ambiguity, he wants to know if he is right. He could ask the man "Are you Dr. Kovacs?" but he does not. Instead he tests his own conclusion by assuming that the man *is* Dr. Kovacs, that his own conclusion *is* correct. Turning to his fellow traveler he asks:

". . . Doctor Kovacs, do you mind if I open the window?"

"Not at all," answered the other. "But tell me, how do you know that I am Doctor Kovacs?"

"It was obvious," replied the scholar.

The Process of Inquiry

Such is inquiry in action. It involves all of the elements described in the preceding chapter—knowledge of the tentative, interpretive nature of knowledge, certain attitudes and values, and a process of inquiring.

This process is extremely important. The folktale used here reveals that there is much more to it than there at first appears to be. It is not a simple set of three or four single steps but a multitude of complex operations. In diagrammatic form, here is what our scholar did:

Main Problem—Who Can It Be?

1. *Sub-problem #1*   *. . . why is he going to Marmaresch?*
   Hypothesize   he's on his way to the . . . wedding. . . .
   Test
   Conclude   No. . . .
   Hypothesize   . . . he's courting. . . .
   Test
   Conclude   No. . . .
   Hypothesize   it's about . . . bankruptcy. . . .
   Test
   Conclude   Yes. . . .

    2. *Sub-problem #2*   *. . . something to do with bankruptcy?*
       Hypothesize   . . . a creditor. . . .
       Test
       Conclude   No. . . .
       Hypothesize   . . . a lawyer. . . .
       Test
       Conclude   Yes. . . .

        3. *Sub-problem #3*   *. . . who could it be?*
           Hypothesize   . . . sister Shprinzah's son. . . .
           Test
           Conclude   No. . . .
           Hypothesize   . . . brother Hayyim's son. . . .
           Test
           Conclude   Yes. . . .

            4. *Sub-problem #4*   *What is his exact name?*
               Hypothesize   . . . must have the title
                                        "Doctor". . . .
               Test
               Conclude   Yes. . . .
               Hypothesize   . . . changed his name to
                                        Kovacs. . . .
               Test
               Conclude   Yes. . . .

Conclusion—In Short, This Is Dr. Kovacs from Budapest!

Then his conclusion is applied to the data to help
make sense out of the situation—and to satisfy the
scholar that his inquiry really is accurate.

This inquiry does not proceed in a uniform, straight line directly from problem to conclusion, but instead its operations double back on each other, occur simultaneously, and sometimes are even omitted. Even negative answers are useful in inquiring. And data—information gathered from books, others' comments, personal observation, and even memory—is most crucial. Careful analysis of this folktale, in sum, ought to help flesh out the concept of inquiry sketched in Chapter 1.

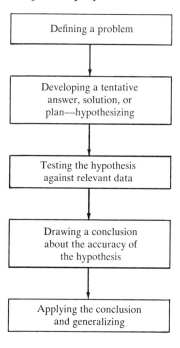

FIGURE 6

Figure 6 illustrates the essential steps of the inquiry process. But there is much more to each of these steps than is evident from this simple diagram. Further analysis of the folktale used here suggests a much more complex but precise model of inquiry. Knowledge of this model is crucial if inquiry teaching is to be at all productive in the classroom.

Defining the Problem

Inquiry starts with an unsettled, discordant, or problematic situation that demands some kind of closure, whether it be in the form of an answer to a question, a solution to a problem, a bit of missing information, or whatever. Not all such situations have to be pointed out to people, nor do they have to be contrived. Life is full of them—they exist ready-made. One need only become aware of them. Once this occurs, and not until, inquiry commences.

The first step is to develop a task or reason for inquiry. This is not as simple as it may appear but involves at least three separate and distinct operations as shown in Figure 7.

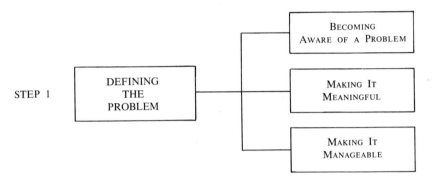

FIGURE 7

What is problematic or unsettled for one individual may very well not be for another. What is a problem to one may not be to another. There are undoubtedly many people on our scholar's train to whom the presence of the lawyer is of no concern at all. Perhaps these people are not naturally curious. Perhaps, since he isn't sitting directly opposite them, he is not relevant to them, and thus his identity poses no problem for them. Or perhaps they have other more pressing problems to think about. At any rate, it is quite likely that the situation described in the foregoing tale cannot have been a part of the lives of most people on that train.

A number of factors contribute to making one aware of a problem. One is its *immediacy*. That is, the closer a discordant situation is to the learner in time, space, or subject matter, the more likely he will be to perceive it as a problem. An amateur geologist recognizing a piece of basalt in a stream bed may ask himself, "How did this get here?" whereas to the average picnicker the presence of the same rock means simply another stone in the stream and suggests no problem at all. What is relevant to one is by no means relevant to another. And even though a situation may be perceived as puzzling, it may not be of concern to the learner because it holds little interest—immediacy or relevancy—for him.

The degree of apparent *discord* in a situation is largely a function of how one perceives a situation. If one does not know the difference between basalt and other rock and does not know that basalt is uncommon to that area, then its presence would not be puzzling. One must know something about a situation in order to become aware of any peculiarity in it. Our scholar, for example, knows enough about Marmaresch to believe that no modern city dweller would want, under normal circumstances, to spend any time there. Yet here is a modern city dweller apparently intending to do just that. To our scholar this doesn't make sense. So his inquiry begins with this puzzle.

On the other hand, if our scholar is not curious, he may never pursue his inquiry to a conclusion. Just because one becomes aware of a problematic situation doesn't mean he will automatically proceed to solve it. The problem must have immediacy, as already noted. It must also be perceived as discordant enough to warrant further investigation but not so complex as to appear impossible to resolve. Whether or not Red China should be admitted to the United Nations may be widely perceived as a problem, but few people may seriously grapple with it because it is either too remote from them or so complex that they feel helpless to deal with it.

Thus, the immediacy (relevance) of and apparent discord within a situation help make one aware of a problem. Both of these in turn depend on the *frame of reference* of the learner. Immediacy and discord have to be perceived by the learner—they are not necessarily inherent in a situation at all. What is "out of order" for one may be perfectly harmonious for another. A person's knowledge, attitudes, and perceptual set or frame of reference shape how he will perceive any given situation. Becoming aware of a problem is a task for the individual inquirer. Until this is done, there is little likelihood of any inquiry taking place.

More than awareness is required, however. Once a problematic situation has been sensed, it must be made meaningful and manageable. It must be cast in terms that have meaning for the inquirer, and it must deal with something that relates to him personally. It must also be easy to handle. The basic question facing our scholar is "Who can it be . . . ?" But this is too big a problem to solve head-on, so he breaks it down into more manageable sub-problems— ". . . why is he going to Marmaresch?" and, when that is solved, ". . . what connection can he have with [bankruptcy] . . . ?" By dealing with each of these in turn, he is able to solve the main problem of the traveler's identity.

Developing a reason for inquiry, therefore, means defining the problem to be investigated. This, in turn, means that at least three things must be done before productive inquiry may be launched—one must become aware of a problematic situation, cast it in meaningful terms, and make it manageable. Once the question is clear, hypothesizing is that much more productive.

Developing a Tentative Answer

The second major operation in inquiring is hypothesizing. A hypothesis is an educated guess—a statement of a possible answer, solution, or alternative that is derived from the learner's past experience and his quick analysis of the present, available data. Hypothesizing is an inductive process—that is, it involves working with separate, often disparate, bits of information and coming up with (inferring) a general statement which apparently explains the proper relationship between all that information and any additional, but as yet unavailable, relevant data. A hypothesis reaches beyond the evidence from which it is derived.

In the folktale referred to above, our scholar is confronted by many bits of data which appear unrelated—a dull, sleepy little town, a number of events underway or about to start there, a well-dressed, professional-looking man, and so on. Once he clarifies the problem, he begins to search for ways in which this data can be related or explained. His statements explaining these ways are his hypotheses.

A hypothesis may result from either intuitive or analytical thinking. Intuition is that flash in the dark, the light bulb over the head in a cartoon, the sudden big idea. It is generally assumed to just pop into our minds. But it does not. An intuitive guess results from some rapid-fire connections in our minds between our perception of the elements of a problematic situation and something we know. An intuitive guess is nothing more than a discovery, and as Bruner has stated, discovery is favored by the well-prepared mind. It doesn't happen in a vacuum.[4]

Thus, a hypothesis may be intuited without any deliberate or systematic thought at all. Our scholar intuits a hypothesis in answer to why his companion is traveling to Marmaresch: "Wait, I've got it! It's about Mottell Kohn's bankruptcy case!" Yet, this is no sudden inspiration pulled out of thin air. It is based on the results of two previous hypotheses that have been discarded and on the knowledge that there is a bankruptcy case in progress at the time.

Intuitive thinking is simply lightning-fast analytical thinking. It may not follow the same orderly procedure as that of analytical thinking, nor may it be conscious and deliberate, but it does involve making connections between the observed data and one's previous experience.

---

[4] Jerome Bruner, *The Process of Education* (Cambridge: Harvard University Press, 1963).

Analytical thinking, on the other hand, is a very deliberate, step-by-step mental manipulation of the evidence. In hypothesizing, we may consciously attempt to analyze the elements of the problematic situation as we perceive it and attempt, by trial and error, to match the various puzzle pieces with our knowledge of the situation. The first time a piece or two matches what we know, we have a hypothesis, a tentative explanation. Our scholar does this, too. His companion is well-dressed—there is going to be a wedding in the town—so perhaps he is going to the wedding. A perfectly reasonable connection—or hunch. Or maybe he is going courting—there are a few eligible girls in the town, and the man appears to be dressed for such an occasion. These hypotheses are not hastily made but rather the result of deliberate yet simple efforts to connect what we perceive to what we know. Hypothesizing thus, whether it be intuitive or analytical, involves a number of separate intellectual operations.

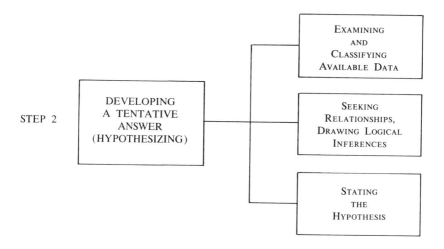

FIGURE 8

Of course this process, illustrated in Figure 8, does not proceed at the same rate of speed for everyone. For some it may require considerable intellectual effort. For others it may be a lightning-quick operation. But it is a crucial step in inquiry, for without it effective learning cannot proceed.

A hypothesis, it must be remembered, is a guess and only a guess. It is not the result or conclusion of inquiry but only a first step. It is simply an inductive inference based on an examination of only fragments of evidence. When we hypothesize, we look at whatever data we have, just as our scholar has done, and then conclude something about that data. Our conclusion may follow from the data, but because our data is so fragmentary, the conclusion does not necessarily have to follow. A hypothesis is a general statement based on incomplete evidence, and it goes beyond that evidence to include other related but as yet unexamined evidence. A hypothesis may be true, but the data from which it is derived is not sufficient to guarantee its absolute validity.

A hypothesis plays a crucial role in inquiring by serving as both a goal and a guide. First, a hypothesis serves as an objective of inquiry, for it tells when the inquiry is ended. If, as in the example used above, further examination of the information about courtship suggests that this is not a reasonable guess, then the hypothesis must be discarded. Our scholar need pursue that particular line of inquiry no further. He knows that the evidence does not substantiate his guess, and he doesn't have to flounder around in a great deal of other information to test it out. Instead, he must make another guess and test it against the data.

Second, a hypothesis serves as a guide for investigating the data relevant to the problem, for it tells which data need be examined and which may be ignored. For example, our scholar's hypothesis that courtship is the reason for this man's trip suggests a need to examine the information about the eligible girls in the community. There is no need to consider anything about job opportunities, vacation spots, or governmental positions, for instance.

A hypothesis is thus a most useful tool. It makes learning efficient because it directs inquiry by telling what kinds of evidence to search out, and it delimits inquiry by setting the goal. Although hypothesizing is absolutely crucial to inquiry, it is by no means the only or final step, however.

Testing the Tentative Answer

A hypothesis is only a tentative answer—a guess or a hunch. Unless it is deliberately tested against all relevant information (or as much information as one can secure in the time available) and is substantiated by this testing, it cannot be considered a final or definitive answer. The process of testing a hypothesis is the key to inquiry. It is here that learning takes place, for it is in doing this that data is located, used, pulled apart, refitted, and manipulated over and over again. It is here that one's creativity, imagination, insight, and accumulated knowledge are brought to bear on a particular situation in order to derive new meaning.

Hypothesis testing involves many tasks. These tasks, as a group, are often described by the terms "analysis" or "analyzing data." However, these terms are so vague and general that they obscure the essence of what occurs when a hypothesis is tested. In reality, this process involves many separate operations, as Figure 9 illustrates.

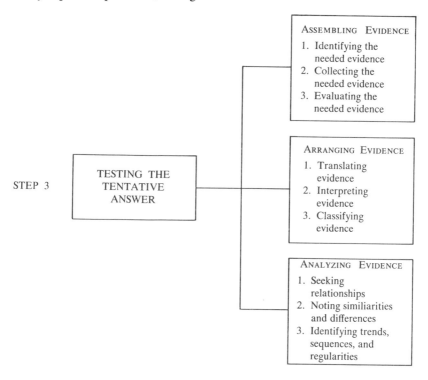

FIGURE 9

The first thing that must be done in testing a hypothesis is to assemble appropriate evidence. This necessitates determining which of all the bits and pieces of obtainable information or data are relevant. Data that is believed to have a bearing on the hypothesis under examination is designated evidence. Before this evidence can be ferreted out, it must be identified. The hypothesis itself serves as the main tool for doing this.

It should be noted here that hypothesis testing is essentially deductive in nature. The term deduction has several meanings. When applied to the process of inquiring, deduction commonly means inferring from general statements—proceeding from the general to the supporting specifics. When applied to logic or reasoning, deduction usually means arriving at a conclusion which follows necessarily from given premises but which does not go beyond those premises.[5] Deduction in both senses is used in this step of inquiring.

In testing hypotheses, we start with a general statement—the hypothesis. Then we move to the supporting specifics. Implicit in every hypothetical statement is the kind of specific evidence that should exist if the statement itself is valid. The task in hypothesis testing is first to infer (deduce) from the statement precisely what this evidence is, then to find it, and finally to authenticate and analyze it. In other words, this step of inquiring is primarily a concerted search for all the evidence needed to guarantee the validity of the particular hypothesis being tested. It is an effort to fill in the gaps in the data from which the hypothesis was induced in the first place so that the statement that logically emerges will not just probably be true—it will of logical necessity have to be true. The hypothesized general statement we start with helps us identify the kind of evidence we need to confirm it. This evidence then leads us to a conclusion that may or may not validate the hypothesis. Our scholar engages in both types of deductive reasoning described here.

This operation commences by drawing out the logical implications of the hypothesis itself. Regardless of the nature of the hypothesis, if it is true, then certain data supportive of it will exist. If, in the case of our scholar, the gentleman on the train is going to Marmaresch to attend a wedding, then there must be someone who is getting married relatively soon. Or, by way of another example, if one has hypothesized that the Civil War was caused by slavery, then one might reasonably expect to find all slave owners and their sympathizers on one side and all non-slave owners and opponents of slavery on the other. The hypothesis thus comes to serve as the tool by which data relevant to its validation is deduced. When cast in this "if . . . then . . ." framework, it tells the inquirer what evidence he needs to substantiate it.

Were it not for this tool, the search for evidence would be an excessively time-consuming, hit-or-miss undertaking. However, knowing the kind of evidence needed tells us what to look for. Knowing that a wedding ought to be scheduled in his town relatively soon if his hypothesis is true, our scholar has only to check the data for the date of the nearest nuptials. Or, knowing that if courtship is the motive for the man's trip to Marmaresch, then there must be some eligible young lady to serve as an attraction. He need only find one.

Knowing the kind of evidence needed may also help us learn where to

---

[5] For a detailed analysis of deduction and induction as processes of inference making see Richard F. Newton, "An Epistemological Critique of the New Social Studies" (Ph.D. diss., Michigan State University, 1969).

look. We exist in a veritable sea of data. We are surrounded by a mass of isolated bits and pieces of information. This data exists in many forms—in books, in newspapers, as still or moving pictures, as cartoons, in advertisements, in diaries and memoirs, in personal letters, in documents, in the form of music or song, in literature and art, as statistics, on maps, in charts, on records, and so on. Only a tiny fraction of it is relevant to the testing of any given hypothesis. Knowing what we are looking for may help us locate which sources of data most likely contain it. If the evidence being sought is a wedding date, for example, then a church calendar or the ledgers of the local marriage license bureau are possible sources.

This evidence may be collected by reading, observing, listening, or other methods. It may even be secured through recall, for the memory of the inquirer himself is certainly a very important data source. For instance, our scholar remembers that although there was a wedding scheduled in Marmaresch, it was yet two weeks away. As a matter of fact, all the evidence used to test our scholar's hypotheses is collected from his own memory or, by observation, from the elements of the situation confronting him. But, regardless of from where or how it is collected, it is collected or assembled for examination. And this is the second step in testing a hypothesis.

Once the evidence has been collected, or more usually as it is being collected, it must be evaluated. The inquirer must determine not only its relevancy to the hypothesis being tested but also its authenticity. That is, each piece of evidence must be examined to determine if it truly is what it purports to be: If a diary, is it really written by its supposed author? If a first-hand newspaper description of an event, is its author writing from personal observation, or did he base it on interviews with those who witnessed it? If a song about work in the mines, is it actually the creation of the mine workers themselves, or was it written by a folk singer and based on his impressions of what work in the mines must have been like? Or, if a statistical chart, what are the sources of the statistics, who collected them, when, and why? Most evidence contains clues to the answers to these and similar questions. Yet many times it is necessary to go beyond the specific piece of evidence under examination in order to answer these questions.

Evaluation also requires determining the accuracy of the evidence. Does the content of the material accurately describe or represent what it is supposed to be about? Do the contents of the diary give dates for events which are historically accurate? Does the newspaper account of the event coincide with other accounts in the basic facts of time and so on? Does the song accurately reflect conditions in the mine as evidenced by perhaps a transcript of a governmental inquiry? Or, do the statistics on a chart correspond with those found in a reputable statistical abstract or almanac?

There are other factors that affect the accuracy of evidence, and these too must be evaluated. The assumptions upon which the evidence is based must be identified. Statements of opinion must be so labeled and distinguished from statements of provable fact. The biases and prejudices of the authors or sources of the evidence must be made explicit—that is, emotionally-charged words and their effect upon the meaning of the evidence as well as any omissions and additions should be noted.

The evidence used must be sufficient as well as accurate. It must include enough cases so that the conclusion is not just probably true but necessarily true. This means that we must deliberately search for enough evidence that, if found, will prove our hypothesis invalid as well as valid. If we don't find any after an honest, thorough search, then our hypothesis stands a greater chance of being valid than it would if we ignored or never searched for such evidence. We cannot validate a guess on skimpy evidence or by ignoring contrary evidence.

Assembling evidence constitutes the first step in hypothesis testing. It consists of three operations—identifying the evidence needed, collecting it, and evaluating it. Our scholar engages in each operation, even if only briefly or by implication, following each hypothesis. Sometimes these operations go on almost simultaneously; at other times they are very deliberately carried out one at a time. Regardless of the order or way in which they are done, they must be done before the evidence thus amassed can be analyzed for its bearing on the hypothesis being tested.

A second set of operations must also be undertaken prior to any attempt to dissect the evidence for meaning. These operations may best be described as *arranging evidence* for analysis. Included here are the operations of translating, interpreting, and classifying evidence. Of course, these do not necessarily occur in this sequence. However, it is essential that they do occur, because it is their function to arrange the evidence for productive analysis.

Translating evidence means exactly that—changing it from one form into another. This may involve preparing a written statement of the contents of a map or of a photograph or of a bar graph. No interpretation is involved here—only the literal reporting of what is seen, heard, read, or experienced.

Interpretation is another completely different operation. Here the apparent meaning of a piece of evidence is summarized or reported. Interpretation must follow translation and should not be confused with it. At one point our scholar hypothesizes that his companion may be a creditor in a bankruptcy case. But in collecting his evidence by observation, he notes that the traveler is smiling, relaxed, and enjoying a newspaper. He interprets his translation of the observed evidence to mean that the man is inwardly calm.

Sometimes it is useful at this stage of hypothesis testing to classify or categorize the evidence into groups, the elements of each of which have certain features in common. There are many types of classification schemes which may be useful including animal–vegetable–mineral, political–intellectual–social–economic–religious, immediate–long-range, past–present–future, and so on. Where a large mass of evidence is to be examined, classifying it into several different categories makes perception of meaningful relationships easier.

Making meaning is the goal of the final stage in hypothesis testing—*analyzing the evidence.* At this point evidence has been searched out and evaluated; it has been translated, if necessary, interpreted, and classified. What remains is to find relationships between the evidence and the hypothesis, to find perhaps similarities and/or differences within the evidence that affect the hypothesis, and to identify trends, sequences, or regularities within this evidence and between it and the hypothesis. These are challenging intellectual operations, but they are the very heart of hypothesis testing.

Our scholar repeatedly analyzes his evidence. After he arranges, translates, and interprets the evidence bearing on his hypothesis that the man in question might be a creditor, he seeks a relationship between this man's apparent behavior and the way he should act if he were a creditor. That is, if the traveler were a creditor and stood to lose some money, then he would be somewhat apprehensive if not downright nervous during the trip to Marmaresch. But he apparently is not. Therefore, at least to our scholar's way of thinking, the necessary relationship between evidence and hypothesis is lacking. Thus, the hypothesis is probably invalid. Similar examples of these activities in operation may be found throughout the description of our scholar's mind at work. They represent the final stage of hypothesis testing.

Hypothesis testing involves considerable analytical thinking. Because such testing involves a very deliberate search for evidence, it is a conscious, purposeful effort. It demands that the inquirer locate all relevant data regardless of its positive or negative bearing on the hypothesis. This data is deliberately pulled apart, examined, and refitted in order to evaluate its supportive or contradictory nature. This is the essence of analytical thinking. It is a much expanded and consciously more deliberate thinking than that used in hypothesizing. Depending on the nature of the hypothesis, it takes considerable time and effort. It also requires one to proceed, in general, through many of the operations described here.

Developing a Conclusion

There is, however, yet another major step in inquiring—that of developing a conclusion. No inquiry would be complete without it, for this is the target toward which an inquirer is motivated by his curiosity and his intolerance of uncertainty. The purpose of inquiring is to bring closure to an unsettled situation. A conclusion, in part, represents that closure.

Developing a conclusion involves basically two operations, as illustrated in Figure 10. First, the inquirer must decide the meaning of what

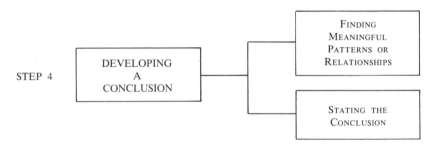

FIGURE 10

he finds in the data as he dissects it. What do the trends, sequences, regularities, and relationships identified in Step 3 mean? What do they mean in themselves, and what do they mean in relationship to the hypotheses being tested? These meanings are the conclusion. Stating them in clear, concise language is the second operation in this step of inquiring.

A conclusion is directly related to the hypothesis being tested. If the concluding statement is merely a restatement of the hypothesis, then we say the hypothesis is valid. But if the concluding statement is not the same, then the hypothesis is invalid. It must be either modified or discarded. Regardless of the outcome, however, the point is that in the process of testing the hypothesis against the evidence, patterns or relationships are perceived which either support, modify, or negate the hypothesis. When these have been stated, a conclusion has been developed.

Our scholar, for example, concludes each phase of hypothesis testing with a brief statement as to the fate of his hypothesis: "But no, that can't be!" "[The wedding is] two weeks off." ". . . he's not going courting." "No, he's not a creditor." "So it stands to reason that the lawyer must be a member of the family." And so on. Finally he states the conclusion of his entire inquiry—"In short, this is Dr. Kovacs from Budapest." This is the answer to the initial question "Who can it be . . .?" Closure has nearly been achieved.

Applying the Conclusion

No conclusion may be considered final or definitive until it has been checked against all the relevant data. The amount and quality of the evidence accumulated and worked with in the process of testing the hypothesis determine the certainty of the conclusion that follows. A conclusion derived from an incomplete sample of relevant data must of necessity be considered more tentative than one tested against all the relevant evidence. The goal of inquiring is to secure all the data needed so that the resulting conclusion will be truly "conclusive."

Ideal as this goal is, achieving it is rarely possible. Seldom can we secure all the evidence needed to derive an absolutely valid general conclusion. Consequently inquiry results many times in a conclusion that, while it is certainly more valid than the initial hypothesis, may still not be perfectly true because all the supportive data needed is simply not available. Such a situation thus compels us to go a step beyond merely developing our own conclusions. Our conclusion may be considered tentative until there arises an opportunity to test it further against the data we are missing. Or, our conclusion may be checked against the findings of others who are considered authorities on the subject under investigation.

Checking a conclusion against what others say is, in fact, a very common way of validating an inquiry—even when we are unfamiliar with how other inquirers arrived at their conclusions. Because we are human we want to know for sure. We want certainty. We also want to be right. We are much more prone to accept as valid conclusions with which we agree than those with which we disagree; we are much more inclined to criticize or submit to careful scrutiny conclusions with which we disagree than those with which we agree. We not only want to know for sure—we want to know we are right!

Regardless of the reasonableness of such inclinations, they exist and directly influence how and why people go about inquiring. People who

engage in inquiry are usually quite reluctant to settle for their own
conclusions as valid ones. They want the satisfaction of "knowing"
absolutely that theirs are correct. Thus they seek the psychological
security of finding others whose investigations substantiate their own.
Only then do they feel comfortable with the results of their inquiry.
Then and only then do they accept their work as valid. Thus, applying
a conclusion to new data—either that which was heretofore missing or
that provided by the work of an accepted authority—is a psychologically
as well as rationally final step in inquiring.

Even our scholar feels a need to substantiate his conclusion. Although
he has carefully figured out the answer to his problem, he still does not
know for sure if he is correct. And he wants to know. So he does in a
roundabout way what he could have done right at the start—he asks
his companion his name. Yet he doesn't ask directly. Instead, he asks:
"Dr. Kovacs, do you mind if I open the window?" He applies what he
thinks is true to the situation before him. And his conclusion is confirmed. His inquiry has been successful. Now he can relax, he has
achieved closure. This was his goal.

Thus, the fifth step of inquiring is a very important one, for it restores
the intellectual and psychological equilibrium which, having been upset,
initiated the inquiry in the first place. When an inquiry involves recorded
data, the conclusion may be applied to new but quite similar data. If it
is substantiated by this data, then it will most likely be accepted as an
established truth. For example, if one investigates why wars come
about—develops a hypothesis as to the causes, tests it against data about
a large number of past wars, and then develops a conclusion about the
causes of wars—he may be fairly well convinced of the accuracy of his
conclusion but will consider it tentative until he can apply it to analyses
of other conflicts such as that in Vietnam. In doing this, he is really
treating his conclusion as a hypothesis and must follow the same process
of testing as he did when testing his original hypotheses. If his conclusion
is validated by this test, he will hold it with more certainty as a general
explanation about the class of data on which it is based—in this instance
about the causes of wars.

One may in the same way test his own conclusions against what the
experts say—against the opinions of recognized authorities who have
investigated the very same problem. In so doing the object is not to
learn that what they say is true but rather to check what the inquirer
himself believes to be true on the basis of his own inquiry with what the
experts feel is true. Again, the inquirer uses his own conclusion as a
hypothesis and tests it against the data provided by the reasoned
opinions of others. Or, he may treat the experts' conclusions as hypoth-

eses to test against the evidence he has uncovered and the conclusions at which he has arrived.

There are times, however, when none of these opportunities present themselves. In these instances a conclusion will be little more than a theory, and the situation will remain somewhat unsettled, as well as psychologically unsettling, until the conclusion can be tested.

Such would have been the situation, for instance, had our scholar been unable to talk with his traveling companion or to otherwise check his identity. His conclusion would have been only a theory at best and only tentative. Such a situation is not easy for many people to live with. But it frequently arises nonetheless. Inquiry does not always move directly to a hard-and-fast, definite answer. Learning to tolerate this uncertainty is sometimes most difficult; but unwillingness to tolerate it forever eventually leads to involvement in the final stage of inquiring.

Applying a conclusion to new data, then, consists of two operations, as Figure 11 outlines.

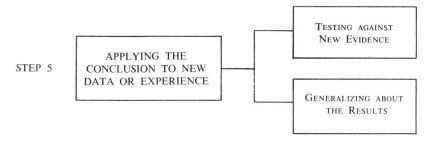

FIGURE 11

Unless one goes through this fifth step, the conclusions reached on the intellectual level must be considered relatively tentative. Only when they have been satisfactorily used to explain new but similar situations or evidence can they be accepted as somewhat definitive. Sometimes conclusions will emerge intact, verified as they stand. Some may even be completely negated. However, it is most likely that they will be altered somewhat in this process. They will almost certainly become more general and less restricted to one particular set of data. Yet they will remain just as useful because they will serve as tools for giving meaning to any similar experience or data encountered in the future.

The process of inquiring is thus quite complex. It is, nevertheless, one very effective way of learning. When viewed as a total operation, it may be conceptualized as in Figure 12.

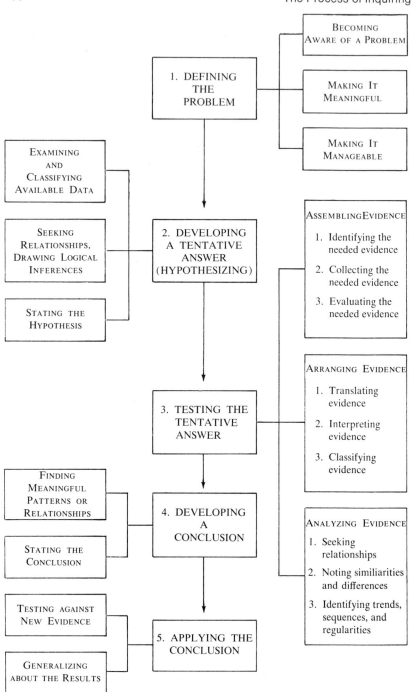

FIGURE 12.   The Process of Inquiring

In essence this process involves three distinct types of intellectual operations—making inferences from data, testing these against more data, and synthesizing bits and pieces of information into meaningful wholes. These operations are performed over and over again in almost every stage of inquiring. In the hypothesizing stage, an inference drawn from a brief survey of the data may be quickly tested and synthesized into a hypothesis. In the testing stage, this hypothesis is examined in the light of new evidence as each aspect is checked and inferences are made about it, tested, and finally refined, retained, or discarded. As in the case of our scholar this same process may be repeated numerous times before any acceptable conclusion is reached. Finally, these same three operations are engaged in when one treats the conclusion as a hypothesis to test it against additional data before finally accepting it— again, as our scholar did in speaking to Dr. Kovacs. These operations form the heart of the inquiry process—but they are not synonymous with it. The process uses these for different reasons and thus encompasses much more.

The process of inquiring, furthermore, utilizes analytical thinking (deliberate, step-by-step, logical thinking) and intuitive thinking (guessing, hunching, jumping to conclusions). Inductive reasoning, moving from bits and pieces of data to all-encompassing statements, and deductive reasoning, moving from all the relevant data to a concluding statement, are also used repeatedly and often interchangeably. Inquiring involves many acts, some conscious and deliberate, others haphazard and almost automatic. It is not always a neat progression of steps from one simple operation to another a bit more complex. The inquirer may frequently go through this process a number of times before the initial problem is resolved. Yet, inquiry starts with a problem or question of some sort and moves at varying rates of speed to some type of a resolution or conclusion. It is one way of making meaning from experience.

A Strategy for Inquiry Teaching

Part 1

Ideally inquiry is self-initiated and self-directed. However, few elementary and secondary school students have either the conceptual framework or intellectual skills required for productive independent inquiry. Their education and training, in school and out, have tended to minimize the development of these skills by concentrating instead on exposition and memorization. It is a purpose of inquiry teaching to remedy this situation by teaching children how to inquire on their own.

Inquiry teaching and inquiry are not identical. Inquiry is a way of learning. Inquiry teaching is teaching by using inquiry. In simple terms, *inquiry teaching is creating and conducting learning experiences which require students to go through the same processes and to develop or employ the same knowledge and attitudes that they would use if they were engaged in independent rational inquiry.*

Although inquiry is learner centered, inquiry teaching requires considerable teacher involvement. Inquiry teaching demands, first, that the teacher plan or design a learning experience that will facilitate student inquiry. This includes creating a series of activities designed to put students through the various stages of inquiry as well as collecting or preparing appropriate learning materials and guides. It also requires that the teacher direct or guide the learning experience by asking questions, making comments or suggestions, and providing data when it is needed. This kind of teacher-directed learning is sometimes referred to as directed or guided inquiry. Regardless of the names applied to it, however, it is inquiry teaching. It is best used to teach students of any grade or ability level how to inquire as they are learning information, developing conceptual knowledge, or clarifying their own attitudes and values. And it may even be used to evaluate how well they can engage in inquiry.

Awareness of these facts of inquiry teaching, however, still does not begin to answer our questions: What can we as teachers do to facilitate inquiry in the classroom, and how can we "bring it off"? What should our strategy be, and what techniques can we use to make it work?

A teaching strategy, as pointed out earlier, is merely a set of techniques arranged to facilitate the attainment of certain objectives. Most strategies are usually described in terms of these techniques—the tangible activities in which the students and teacher engage. What is supposed to happen in the mind of the learner is, at best, only vaguely implied and usually not at all evident.

A strategy for inquiry teaching is different. This kind of teaching cannot be planned by trying first to decide what content to cover, which pages to assign, what monologue to give, or what film to show. It can only be conducted by continuous and conscious reference to the specific mental operations in which the learners should engage. Since it is used to facilitate learning by inquiring, an inquiry-teaching strategy must describe explicitly the intellectual operations which productive inquirers customarily use.

An effective strategy of inquiry teaching is built directly on inquiry itself. Such a strategy is an outline of what the learner does in his mind rather than a list of instructional activities or techniques. There are undoubtedly a number of ways to describe such a strategy, but its essential elements may be outlined as shown in Figure 13. This is a basic strategy for inquiry teaching. It cannot be described in terms of the instructional techniques by which it is made operational in the classroom, for every single item in our repertoire of teaching techniques may be used to facilitate inquiry. There certainly is a place for the textbook in inquiry teaching, for example, and for the sound film and the oral report. But not as ends in themselves. It is how these are arranged and used that determine the degree to which the learning experience which they facilitate is inquiry oriented. To make decisions as to why, how, and when certain techniques should be employed to promote inquiry, we must know precisely what it is that the students are supposed

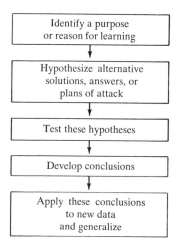

FIGURE 13

to be experiencing in their minds. Knowledge of and reference to a strategy such as the one outlined here are thus essential to effective inquiry teaching.

In using inquiry teaching in the classroom, we must remember that the main goal is to facilitate learning—not to tell the students what they are supposed to be learning. Our task as teachers is to design learning experiences which stimulate this inquiry in a structured, meaningful way. Thus, the main task in planning for inquiry teaching is one of translation—selecting instructional techniques and arranging them in such a way as to engage the students in the desired mental activity. This requires constant reference to the essential stages of a strategy for inquiry teaching.

Identifying
a Purpose for Learning

Inquiry grows out of curiosity or a felt need to know something. It has a specific purpose. This purpose may be stated in the form of a question which requires an answer, a problem which needs a solution, a perplexing situation which begs to be unraveled, or a curiosity that demands satisfaction. Or it may be to test an already formulated hypothesis, to check someone else's conclusions against available data, or to examine the evidence used by a particular person to test his own hypothesis. Whatever its form, a purpose guides and sustains the entire learning experience. Without it there will be little inquiry and little learning.

Consequently, the first job in inquiry teaching is to develop a purpose for inquiring.

There are several ways in which a purpose may be developed. Teachers commonly present a purpose to their students in the form of a question to answer or a problem to solve. Although this is a practical way to initiate student inquiry along lines which we can plan in detail and control, it may lead to very little real learning.

Teacher-given problems are frequently little more than traditional textbook topics cast in the form of a question. How many students are turned on or enthused by questions such as: Was Louis XIV a divine-right monarch? or Why did Jackson veto the bank? These are our problems, not the students'. Such problems hardly appear relevant to them. Yet most students will move to resolve them if for no other reason than to please us or to live up to what is expected of them or to avoid a tongue-lashing or, even worse, a failing grade.

Student involvement in learning initiated in this manner may be quite half-hearted to say the least. The student usually has little desire to resolve the initial problem because it really doesn't bother him anyway. What motivation there may be is largely external to him. Consequently, his commitment to achieving rational closure is likely to be rather minimal and the resultant learning most superficial.

Another way in which to initiate inquiry is to allow the students to generate a purpose of their own. The most productive learning, in fact, starts with student-initiated problems or questions, for such a purpose assumedly has some meaning for them. As a result they are more likely to feel that the purpose requires fulfillment, and they will be more highly motivated to achieve their goals. Students, in dealing with their own purposes, exhibit much greater involvement in and commitment to achieving closure than they do in trying to resolve those of others. Consequently more and better learning occurs.

This approach, however, is more suited to evaluating how well students can inquire than it is to teaching them how to inquire. Although it leads to more effective learning than the previous approach, it is in many ways quite impractical. Inquiry teaching demands extensive use of data. Allowing students to select topics of inquiry means that teachers must have or be able to secure quickly sufficient audio, visual, and written materials to make investigation into any chosen topic possible. Most of us are not in this happy situation. Instead, we must anticipate the kinds of data that will be needed so we can ensure its availability or so we can steer the students into an area of inquiry where sufficient data is known to exist. To do this we must know the kinds of hypotheses most likely to be in need of testing, and this means knowing the problem that will give rise to these hypotheses.

In addition, most teachers are required or feel obligated to teach a specific syllabus. This generally means working with a certain body of content in a given number of weeks. Many of us feel we cannot do this if we permit students to select anything at all as the subject of study. Regardless of the arguments for or against such a belief, this is an important consideration in inquiry teaching. In order to conduct a worthwhile inquiry-teaching experience, to fulfill our responsibilities to the school and students, and to capitalize on what is known about effective learning, we, as teachers, should be able in some way to direct the data or content that is going to be used. The best way to ensure this control is by helping, or perhaps guiding, the students as they shape a purpose for inquiring.

There are thus two basic teaching tasks involved in developing a purpose for effective inquiry—choosing an initiatory problem that is relevant to the students and focusing on an area of investigation in which sufficient data is or will be immediately available to the students. Neither of the approaches suggested thus far accomplishes both of these tasks.

A more useful approach represents a combination of the essential elements of these two techniques. The initiatory problem may be presented *indirectly* by the teacher—not in the form of a question to be answered but rather in the form of a situation that will create a question or perplexity in the minds of the students which they will want to resolve. In this way we may delimit the nature of the topic to be investigated, will know in advance the kinds of data most likely needed, and can plan accordingly. And the students, when confronted with such a situation, will have the satisfaction of articulating a problem or question relevant to them. Thus, the learning experience that follows will be motivated by a desire to solve their own problem, not ours, and will be more likely to lead to very enthusiastic, productive learning.

Inquiry teaching may be initiated with any of several different kinds of problem-type situations. The students may be presented with (1) an unpopular argument about a topic in which they are known to be quite interested, (2) several conflicting opinions on the same subject, (3) material which contradicts the biases or stereotypes held by the students, or (4) an incomplete, mystery-type situation which fairly begs for a solution. An example of each of these follows.

An Unpopular Argument

Let us assume that we wish our students to develop or refine a concept of multiple causation while at the same time develop their skills of intellectual inquiry. Let us also assume that we want to use content about wars in American history. Finally, let us assume that we know our students, especially the boys who are rapidly approaching draft age, are quite concerned about or at least interested in the Vietnam conflict. To initiate the study of this unit, we could present, without comment, a cartoon, quotation, picture, or recorded statement that expresses some kind of opinion about why the United States became engaged in the fighting in Vietnam. In examining this piece of data, some students will make an evaluative comment about it—"This is trash!" "I agree!" "Who said this?" "How could anyone believe that?" "Is this for real?" and so on. We or the class may single out several of these comments and have them explained. Class reaction to this data will initiate an investigation of why and how the United States got involved in Vietnam, and this investigation, in turn, can lead into an inquiry-oriented study of American wars in general and their causes in particular. In beginning a study in this fashion, we thus deliberately play on something we know is relevant to the students; we give them a piece of material which will lead them into a specific body of content so we can have the appropriate data ready for them to use. The students, by reacting to this piece of material, will articulate something of concern to them which can serve as the initiatory problem for the entire study. This technique—giving students a statement designed to evoke a student-initiated line of inquiry which can lead into a conceptual study using predetermined content—may be used to initiate an inquiry study of any number of content areas.

Conflicting Opinions

Another way in which we may create a problematic situation is to present the students with two conflicting views of the same subject. For example, to initiate a study of decision making by examining the careers of a number of world political leaders, we might present to the students two conflicting statements about the abilities of a particular leader:

I	II
Abraham Lincoln was a man of high ideals. He believed in the equality of all men. He saw the Civil War as an opportunity to free the Negroes from human bondage. His Emancipation Proclamation was the most humane act of any American president.	There was no greater political opportunist in 19th century America than Abraham Lincoln. His entire public career was one of making deals and playing politics. When it was convenient for him, he favored slavery. When it was not, he opposed it. Freeing the slaves was purely a political move. Lincoln had no real feeling for Negroes as people.

Which is correct? Who wrote these? When were these written? These and similar questions are quite likely to be raised as these statements are read. When they are, the inquiry may be launched. And it will be the students who do it.

The same technique may be done with pictures—paintings, slides, photographs, movies, or so on. If we wish to initiate a study of social class by studying Latin America, for instance, we might display a montage of magazine pictures or advertisements of the colorful night life, crowded beaches, beautiful buildings, and busy streets of Rio de Janeiro along with another montage of pictures of the shanty slums, lines of unemployed, beggars, and ill-clothed children of that same city. Students will almost immediately identify a problem that they perceive, and the inquiry will thus be underway.

A point should be made here about using statements and even pictures or recordings in this manner. If the objective is to start inquiring about the content represented by the initial material, its author or source need not be indicated. Written statements need not even be authentic; that is, a teacher may contrive them in order to sharpen the points of conflict to be raised. On the other hand, if the objective is something other than a study of certain content—perhaps to analyze how a frame of reference may affect one's interpretation of reality—then the author's name or source of the quotes, pictures, or recording must be available.

This particular technique is very effective in launching an inquiry-teaching experience. The use of written statements, such as the preceding statements about Lincoln, is perhaps best suited to average or above-average secondary school students. But use of pictures or recordings may serve the same purpose with below-average secondary school students or students in the elementary grades. The point is that the substance of this initial material is not to be remembered or "learned"—it is only a situation in which the students may perceive a problem that they would like, or at least be willing, to resolve.

Material Contradictory to Student Biases

A third type of problematic situation may be created by presenting the students with material that dramatically contradicts their biased or stereotyped view of the topic to be studied. Most students, for example, have a Tarzan-like image of Africa south of the Sahara. To them it is full of jungles, wild animals, grass huts, diamonds, and black, naked people who are either under four feet or over seven feet tall! One way to start an inquiry-oriented study of Africa would be to confront the students with a series of two kinds of photographs—pictures of what they think is typically African (the stereotyped image) and pictures of things these students do not associate with Africa but which really are African (large cities, steel mills, jet airliners, high speed railways, sidewalk cafes, department stores, night clubs, football stadiums, apartment houses, tractors, gangplows, factories, and the like). If challenged to pick out the pictures taken in Africa, the students will tend to select those which conform to their stereotyped views. When confronted with the fact that all have been taken in Africa, they will protest: "It's a trick!" "Prove it!" "I don't believe it; Africa doesn't have modern cities!" "These are exceptions." As the students go on to articulate their views and to search for data to support them, the inquiry experience will be launched. Again, we can delimit the area of study, but the students themselves come up with a reason for studying this subject.

A Mystery-type Situation

Still another way to initiate an inquiry-teaching experience is to present the students with an open-ended, mystery-type situation which bothers them into seeking a solution. An unfinished case study may be a very useful piece of material to use in this kind of introduction. Here the students read about or see a specific situation but do not find out how it is or was resolved. To introduce a unit on the political process in which the conceptual objectives relate to leadership or decision making, we might, for example, show the film *True Story of an Election*[6] which traces the events and campaigns of two contenders for a Congressional seat but stops just after the votes have been cast and before the winner is known. This is comparable to stopping Perry Mason just before he announces "who did it" and why. Motivated by their own natural desire for closure—to know the answer, to bring certainty out of uncertainty—the students will ask the kind of questions needed to launch a productive, inquiry-oriented learning experience.

Another kind of technique that can be used in this way is the "discovery exercise." Students may be presented with some uninterpreted material, such as several paintings, for instance, or some graphs showing different aspects of the same subject, or a list of words, or some statistics, or even several newspaper headlines and dates. If the material is on a familiar topic but does not quite make sense, the students may want to know "What is this?" Such a question is really a statement of the problem. Or the students may imply a problem statement by trying to interpret the material. With this statement, inquiry is launched.

---

[6] Produced by Churchill Films, 662 North Robertson Blvd., Los Angeles, California 90069.

These are but four ways to help students develop a purpose for learning. They may be used to initiate inquiry teaching in a wide variety of content areas and for any conceptual, affective, or skill objectives. All of these are designed to tantalize the mind, to tempt further inquiry. They are built on the fact that people desire closure, that most have a low tolerance for ambiguity and uncertainty.

It must be remembered, however, that inquiry teaching does not trick students into inquiring. It does not use gimmicks to get the students to study about things that have little apparent interest to them. Worthwhile learning occurs only when students feel that the whole experience warrants their attention. They must believe it is relevant to their needs or interests, or they will not allow themselves to be "tricked" again.

The best way to initiate inquiry teaching is thus to use the students' own experiences and psychological sets to induce them to want to inquire. The material used to initiate learning must have a legitimate and direct relationship to the content and objectives of the planned study. It must be a natural lead-in. It must be such that any problem or question that arises out of it will lead into the area of content the teacher desires the students to study, and it must also be such that it permits the students to conceive a problem of their own.

The purpose of this phase of inquiry teaching is to stimulate students to raise questions, to identify problems that bother them. Many students, especially those in the secondary grades, are quite reluctant to do this and may need, at least at first, considerable guidance and direction. These may be provided in the first instance by teacher-created opportunities for the students to identify problems for study that relate to one or more of their own concerns or interests. Some techniques for providing these opportunities have been suggested here. Students' responses to these situations ("What is this?" "Which is correct?" "Who said that?" "This can't be true!") all state or imply student-generated problems that merit attention.

Identifying an area of concern is only the first step in developing a reason for inquiring. Before students can go about solving a problem effectively, the problem itself must be quite clear. Thus, once a statement such as those cited above is produced and consensus warrants looking into it, the students must clarify the essential nature of the task to be undertaken. This means making the problem meaningful and manageable.

Clarifying the problem does not require that we resolve it. It simply requires that we ask the students questions designed to make them state the problem as simply and directly as possible. We may ask, "What do you mean by that?" or say, "Explain what you have in mind." If, for example, the students after examining the different pictures on Africa respond with "This can't be true!" then we must ask "Why?" and the dialogue may proceed something like this:

STUDENTS: "Because Africa doesn't have big cities or factories or department stores like these."

TEACHER: "What do you think it has?"

STUDENTS: "Jungles—small villages of grass huts—natives hunting wild game—uncivilized tribes constantly warring against each other. . . ." (This is a hypothesis.)

TEACHER: (Wishing to clarify the problem to be investigated before proceeding to test the hypothesis): "We seem to have several different ideas about Africa."

STUDENTS: "Well, what's the answer? What is Africa really like."

Here is the problem statement, articulated by the students. The teacher may return to his first question ("What do you think?"), treat the answer as a hypothesis, and proceed with the inquiry. Or he may see a need for clarifying the problem further. He may, for instance, insist on defining the words "really" and "Africa." Does Africa mean the entire continent, only the lands south of the Sahara, black nations only or also Rhodesia and South Africa, independent nations or also areas under foreign control? It is absolutely essential to effective inquiry that ambiguous words, terms, or phrases be identified and defined in the context of the situation and that the problem be stated in the words of the students themselves.

It is also important that the problem be made manageable. This requires that the large problems such as: What caused the Civil War? What's new about the "new" Social Studies? What is Africa really like? be broken down into a number of related, smaller questions, the answer to each of which will provide clues to the resolution of the basic problem. The problem about Africa, for example, might be broken down into several smaller problems such as: What are the people like who live south of the Sahara? What are the African climates like? Where do Africans live? and so on. Regardless of the specific questions devised, the more specific the problem and the more clearly it is stated, the more easily it may be resolved. Making problems, once identified, specific and clear is the task of the students but may require varying amounts of teacher guidance. And this teacher guidance is provided by asking questions—not answering them!

It is tempting and sometimes necessary, especially when first using this strategy in the classroom, to ask the students a question when presenting them with a problematic situation. We may give the students two conflicting statements about the same thing and then ask, "Which is correct?" Or when we show pictures of Africa we may ask, "Which are most accurate?" But in so doing, we are really handing students the problem to solve and thus doing the very thing that this introductory technique is designed to circumvent. The best learning requires student-perceived and articulated purposes. The first stage in inquiry teaching is facilitating, not obviating, the development of such purposes.

Developing
a Tentative Solution

Once a reason for inquiry has been sharply defined and stated in manageable terms, inquiry may proceed. The next operation is one suggesting alternative solutions or formulating tentative answers—hypothesizing. To hypothesize is to guess using all immediately available data whether it be contained in written, audio, or visual media or in the memories of the students themselves. This is essentially an inductive process since it proceeds from bits and pieces of data to a generalized statement that seems to explain some relationship between these and the initiatory problem. The process also involves both deliberate, step-by-step analysis and intuitive hunching. It may require considerable intellectual effort to arrive at a tentative explanation, or one may just suddenly "pop up."

Hypothesizing is an essential part of inquiring, for a hypothesis serves to guide further inquiry. It is not a final answer but only a tentative one. It is generally developed by a rather quick and often almost intuitive examination of the available data. Sometimes it even precedes a clearly defined statement of the problem being investigated.

The ideal hypothesizing experience is one which is student directed, in which each class member formulates his own hypothesis and knows that his guess is only a tentative answer and that it is quite likely to change. Planning for such an experience and guiding one to fruition are major tasks in inquiry teaching.

Data is an important ingredient in the hypothesizing experience. Students cannot hypothesize without it—even intuitively. The necessary data may be provided by the teacher, it may be contained in the problematic situation that initiated the problem under investigation, or it may be presented in some other form as soon as the students have decided on a problem to examine. Or, appropriate data may already exist in the mind of the student, for every student's past experience has provided him with information and concepts that may be brought to bear in forming hypotheses. Indeed, it is generally true that such student-supplied data is always used in hypothesizing whether or not the teacher realizes it. That is why a number of students can look at the same teacher-supplied data in an effort to answer the same question but quite legitimately come up with different hypotheses. Remember, the information used by our scholar in trying to identify his traveling companion came from his background of experience, not from any library.

If we are preparing the students to attack a problem on an individual basis, the fact that each student generates a different hypothesis would not be disturbing at all. But if we want to conduct the subsequent investigation as a class activity with all students testing the same hypothesis, then we are faced with a problem. One way to deal with this problem is to provide the students with very specific, controlled data. Such provision may not totally eliminate a variety of guesses, but it tends to focus all attention on a very definite channel and usually leads most students in the class to formulate the same general hypothesis.

Such an accomplishment requires, of course, considerable direction. This direction can be supplied best by questions or comments which require the students to focus on certain parts of the data or which challenge hastily-made student inferences. Combining a teacher-directed experience with highly controlled data may to a large degree lead most of the students to formulate the same general hypothesis. Moreover, it may also teach students how to develop hypotheses analytically by examining available data, identifying trends and similarities, seeking relationships, drawing significant inferences from these operatons, and preparing a statement which gives meaning to all.

Perhaps the techniques of teacher-directed hypothesizing can be illustrated by briefly examining the way in which one piece of instructional material is designed to be used. The material is a transparency with multiple overlays on the subject of late nineteenth-century imperialism.[7] It is intended to serve as the basis for a very highly teacher-controlled, one-day lesson.

The students are first confronted with a number of statements which are reasons given for securing colonies in the late nineteenth century. They are directed by the teacher to identify the key words in each statement and then to formulate these into an all-encompassing statement. However these reasons are highly selective—they each reflect some

---

[7] *European Imperialism in Africa 1871–1914,* 12 overhead transparencies–#30051 (Chicago: Encyclopedia Britannica Films, Inc., 1964).

kind of economic reason. And it is the economic terms in each statement that the students are to identify and explain as the key elements. Thus, the only possible statement students can develop by way of synthesis is an economic explanation for imperialism. This becomes the hypothesis. The lesson then continues on to test this hypothesis against highly selective economic data, eventually to cast serious doubt on this as a valid hypothesis, and to lead the students to formulate another, possibly more viable hypothesis to test.

It is quite obvious that this material intends to teach students a very deliberate process of hypothesizing. But because it does not encourage—indeed, it attempts to eliminate—divergent or creative thinking on the part of the students using their own frames of reference, it is extremely restrictive. Nevertheless, it is one way to go about creating hypothesizing experiences in inquiry teaching. It would probably be quite appropriate in the early stages of inquiry teaching when teaching students how to hypothesize, but it would not be appropriate to use after they had become familiar with some essential steps in hypothesizing.

Such an approach might also be used when the students have very little if any previous knowledge to apply when hypothesizing about a particular problem. Thus in order to permit inquiry to continue in productive channels, we teachers might give the students some information to help them hypothesize. The material described above might be used if the students knew nothing at all about imperialism. Whether or not we would become as highly involved as suggested above would depend, however, on the degree to which the students knew how to handle such data. The students could be handed the statements on imperialism, for example, and left alone to formulate their own hypotheses. In this case we would not attempt to intrude on or direct their thinking at all. This strategy brings us to another ingredient of hypothesizing—asking questions.

A hypothesis is the answer to a question or several questions. These questions may be explicitly stated or merely implied. The hypothesis about imperialism being caused by economic reasons, for example, is an answer to the implied question, "What causes imperialism?" And the statement that Africa is a land of jungles, small villages of grass huts, and so on is in answer to "What do you think it (Africa) has?" Ideally these questions should be asked by the students, but because they may be unaccustomed to asking such questions, they must be taught how. We may have to lead them to ask these kinds of questions or perhaps even pose the questions ourselves until the students learn how and when to do so. Inquiry teaching must teach students how to inquire, especially how to ask useful questions of experience.

It is neither necessary nor desirable, however, for the teacher to strictly direct all hypothesizing activities. The immediate task in inquiry teaching at this point is to teach students the necessity of hypothesizing, of stating a hypothesis and using it. It is not necessary to teach a step-by-step process, for this is better taught when hypothesis testing is taught. Hypothesizing ought to be a creative endeavor, postulating connections between the initiatory problem and some already known data. In doing this the student should be free to use his imagination, free to engage in divergent thinking, even free to be irrational!

One way to help students hypothesize is for us to provide, if necessary, some data which may be useful to them and then step out of the way. If the students have elected to find out what Africa is really like by trying to find out what Africans themselves are like, they might select several different ethnic groups to study. Any American elementary school student has some impressions of what Africans are like and can easily hypothesize about them. Yet we can make this study more productive by providing some information for the students, such as some paintings of one group, some folklore of another, or even a selection of words from the language of a third group. The students already have a problem—"What are Africans themselves like?"—and now they have something to supplement their personal impressions. No teacher is really needed to guide them in postulating tentative answers to their question.

We may find it necessary, at least at first, to do several other things, however. Students may need encouragement to guess at possible answers and to identify alternative solutions. They must ask such questions as "How would you account for this?" or "What might be a reason for this?" or "What might help explain this?" It may be necessary to push them into speaking out.

Different types of students tend to react differently, at least at first, to hypothesizing situations. Average and below-average students tend to be good hypothesizers because most of the "answers" they give in class are hypotheses. These students are often accustomed to being wrong so they have no fear of guessing. Honor students, on the other hand, are frequently very reluctant to guess because their grades were achieved by giving correct answers—not by hypothesizing. Many hesitate to volunteer until they are certain their answers are correct or what they think the teacher wants. Frequently these students must be strongly encouraged to hypothesize.

Reluctant hypothesizers can sometimes learn to "open up" by formulating and testing statements about what something is not. Students are often more willing to guess at negative possibilities than to hypothesize about a correct answer. By testing these negative possibilities, that is, by trying to prove that something is not what they think it is not, they may in the process determine what it really is. This approach affords students considerably less chance of embarrassing themselves since they need not put their knowledge on the line. And, at the same time, they also learn a very valuable research technique.

We may also find it necessary to remind students that their answers at this point are nothing more than guesses, that they cannot be accepted as correct without further testing or corroboration. Students must be prevented from treating a hypothesis as the answer. "How do you know?" is the kind of question that can point out this fault just as can "What makes you say that?" In many classrooms what passes for inquiry is merely hypothesizing, but hypothesizing is not the end result.

It should be noted here, too, that the widely held fear that students, if left to themselves, may come up with the "wrong" hypothesis is really unwarranted. There is no such thing as a wrong hypothesis. A hypothesis may be irrelevant to the problem or inappropriate in the sense that the data needed to test it is not available, but it cannot be wrong. A hypothesis is not an answer—it is a guess at an answer. It is not an end product of inquiry but a search tool by which inquiry is facilitated. Rightness or wrongness is determined by the test of the evidence. A "wrong" hypothesis is an impossibility—a contradiction in terms.

Sometimes student hypotheses appear to be wild guesses. The normal teacher reaction is to stare down such a guess, ignore it, or perhaps even ridicule it. Yet such a guess may very well serve to initiate useful inquiry. It is not uncommon for some students to answer the question "Who was the general who won the battle of Waterloo?" with a guess such as "Charlemagne!" Rather than belittling such hasty guessing, we could proceed with this:

TEACHER: "What makes you say that?"

STUDENT: "I dunno. . . . He's a famous general. . . ."

TEACHER: "How can we determine if you are correct?"

STUDENT: "Look it up in the textbook!"

TEACHER: "How?"

STUDENT: "Find 'Waterloo' in the book and see who it says won."

A quick glance through the index will enable the students to check and discover that Charlemagne did not win that battle. At the same time it will give a good hint as to who did. Thus, a student who often proposes wild guesses will begin to gain insight into the skills of hypothesizing, of using a text, of drawing inferences from data and he will not be ridiculed out of the entire learning situation. Moreover it will be the data that disproves his hypothesis—not a statement by the teacher. Hypotheses in themselves may sometimes be wild guesses—but never "wrong."

The same must be kept in mind when considering what to do if a student offers the correct answer as his hypothesis. To some this might mean that the whole planned experience is ruined before it begins. But a correct answer in no way invalidates the planned inquiry nor does it require that it be abandoned. Such a response must be treated merely as any other possible answer to the problem under investigation—it should be subjected to further proof. For the student who already knows he is correct, this testing may provide an opportunity to learn new skills, to work with new information, to help others inquire, and to develop or refine additional knowledge. It will also provide an opportunity for him to study further data against which to check his hypothesis. It is possible for students to think they know when, in fact, they really do not. So it is important that even though a hypothesizer "knows" or suspects that his hypothesis is the only one that will stand the test of the data, he must treat it just like all the others and submit it to testing. It is in the process of verifying guesses that new substantive learning occurs, and this, after all, is the object of inquiry teaching.

A
Strategy
for
Inquiry Teaching

4

Part 2

The process of inquiring consists of a number of distinct intellectual operations. Two of these operations set the stage for new learning: identifying a purpose—possibly a problem—for learning and developing a tentative solution to this problem. Although these two steps are part of inquiring, they are preliminary to the actual production of new insights or meanings. It is the remaining steps of inquiring that actually produce new knowledge—the steps of testing the hypothesis, developing a conclusion, and applying the conclusion to new data. Of all these operations, hypothesis testing is probably the most complicated, and also the most crucial.

Testing
the Hypothesis

Hypothesis testing or examining the alternative solutions to a problem is the third major step in inquiring and hence in inquiry teaching. It is here that new learning takes place, for it is in doing this that we come into contact with new information—dissecting it, rearranging it, and pulling it apart over and over again. It is here that our creativity, imagination, and past experience are brought to bear on what we already know in order to develop new meanings. Such mental manipulation of information leads not only to familiarity with the information itself but also to the development of conceptual knowledge, a major cognitive objective of inquiry teaching.

For purposes of analysis, we can separate hypothesis testing into three basic steps—assembling evidence, arranging evidence, and analyzing evidence. In order for students to inquire effectively, they must know these general steps. They must also know the more precise operations of which each of these steps consists. If students are to develop a systematic way of testing hypotheses, they must be put through learning activities that focus on each of these steps. Of course, it is not necessary nor is it even desirable in inquiry teaching to give equal attention to each step in every lesson, for this would be stifling to say the least. Instead, different lessons should emphasize different operations so that over a period of time students will gain enough practice to be able to conduct every operation on their own.

The operations which constitute hypothesis testing do not always proceed in any set sequence. Nor does one operation wait on the completion of others. Far from it. As we collect information to analyze, we also frequently make judgments about its validity and authenticity. We may even translate and interpret it simultaneously. We might arrange and analyze a small amount of data before assembling more. Hypothesis testing is not necessarily a one-at-a-time series of steps. It is a very complex process. Nevertheless, separation of hypothesis testing into its three basic operations is useful for a better understanding of this step of inquiry teaching.

Assembling Evidence

The first step in testing a hypothesis is to assemble the necessary evidence. In order to do this, however, we must determine what kind of evidence is needed and where it can be found. Reference to our hypothesis can help us accomplish both of these tasks.

The hypothesis being tested plays a dual role in this step of inquiry. Its validation serves as the target towards which the testing proceeds. At the same time, the hypothesis helps determine which of all the information or data available to us may be used as evidence. The term evidence implies much more than data supportive of the hypothesis. *Evidence is information that in some way has a bearing on that hypothesis.* It may be data that tends to support the hypothesis, or it may be data that invalidates it. Both kinds of information must be sought out and analyzed if a hypothesis is to be properly tested.

The hypothesis itself directs the search for evidence. Once students have formulated a clearly defined hypothesis, they should proceed to identify its logical implications in terms of the kinds of evidence that ought to exist if the hypothesis is valid. This identification may be managed by constructing an "if . . . then . . ." statement.[8] If the hypothesis is true, then certain evidence will exist to prove it. If the hypothesis is true, then also certain evidence which might invalidate it—that which is opposite the supportive evidence—will not exist.

For example, if students have hypothesized that a certain people are Moslem, they might suggest the following implications of their hypothesis for data-gathering purposes:

If these people are Moslem, *then*:

> they will have mosques.
> they will pray five times daily.
> they will study and quote the *Koran.*
> the Sabbath day will be Friday.
> . . . and so on.

Having made such inferences, the students now know what kinds of evidence will help them validate their hypothesis. But this "if . . . then . . ." statement also suggests the kinds of evidence that, if found, will invalidate the hypothesis:

If these people are Moslem, *then*:

> they will not have temples, synagogues, or cathedrals.
> they will not study or quote the *Bible* or *Torah.*
> the Sabbath day will not be Saturday, Sunday, or Monday.
> . . . and so on.

If we expect to find mosques, we do not expect to find synagogues, temples, or great cathedrals. If we expect to find the *Koran* in use, we do not expect to find widespread use of the *Bible, Torah,* or writings of Confucius. Should these latter items be found instead of the *Koran* or mosques, then the accuracy of the hypothesis will be in doubt. Should only the former be found, then the hypothesis may be valid. Thus, the "if . . . then . . ." statement is crucial for it implies not only the kind of evidence which should exist if the hypothesis is true but also the kind of evidence that should not exist. No hypothesis testing is complete until both kinds of evidence have been deliberately sought out.

---

[8] The role of this operation in inquiry has been carefully delimited, especially in its theoretical import, by a number of scholars, foremost among whom are Maurice P. Hunt and Lawrence Metcalf, *Teaching High School Studies* (New York: Harper & Row, 1955), pp. 79–87. See also 2nd ed., pp. 221–236.

As the search for data and its evaluation proceeds, the teacher must see to it that the hypothesis is constantly referred to. He must deliberately guide the students by asking such questions as, "If your hypothesis is true, then what kind of evidence do you need or expect to find?" or "What would you look for to prove your hypothesis?" until they learn how to draw out the logical implications of their hyptheses.

Suppose that the students have hypothesized that people in Latin America live where they do because of the accessibility of water. They will then have to deal with a series of questions such as:

1. If your hypothesis is true, then in what parts of Latin America would you expect to find large concentrations of people?
2. Where do you find the large concentrations of people which you expected to find?
3. Where should you find large concentrations of people, according to your hypothesis, but cannot? How do you account for this?
4. Where do you find large concentrations of people that are not where you expected them to be? How do you account for this?

These questions, oral or written, may be provided by the teacher for those who are just learning to inquire. However, they must ultimately originate with the students. Answering them may be study activities designated for the class, a small group, or an individual. Whatever the designation, considerable information will be needed—data about population distribution and density, elevation, rainfall, location of rivers and lakes, distribution of urban areas, transportation networks, climate regions, vegetation zones, and soil types.

Identifying possible sources of data is the second requisite for assembling evidence. Data may be communicated in a variety of forms. It may be pictorial, statistical, audio, or written. If written, it may be found in maps, charts, newspapers, letters, diaries, novels, documents, monographs, and even textbooks. It may be contained in speeches, lectures, interviews, folk stories, and casual conversation. It may be in the form of physical remains or objects. There are many possible media to which a student may turn for the evidence he seeks.

It is important that students come to know and use these media so they can learn to identify what sources will most likely contain what evidence. In searching for data relevant to whether or not a certain people are Moslem, students might reasonably decide that current photographs or a first-hand account of life with these people by a famous anthropologist are the best sources to consult. If they can find pictures, they will need to look for mosques, people praying in large groups, school children studying the *Koran,* and so on. If they can find a relevant anthropological study, they will seek written descriptions of the religion of these people, of Moslem mosques, or of religious ceremonies. In searching for data to test the hypothesis about population distribution in Latin America, students might turn to an atlas. If they find people clustered near rivers, lakes, and along the coasts, their hypothesis may be valid. But if they find large population clusters great distances from water, their hypothesis may be quite invalid. Students need to know where to find evidence and how to use of data. This knowledge is an important dimension of inquiry.

Once students have identified the kinds of evidence needed and the sources where most likely it can be found, they must be given opportunities to collect it. Collecting evidence may involve two separate operations—locating the source of the data and finding the appropriate evidence in that source. Teaching students how and where to locate useful and reliable sources may be accomplished by sending them to the library or study center to seek, without direction, pictures, magazine or newspaper clippings, reference works, textbooks, films, or other media which might contain pertinent evidence. If the students have had no training in how to use the *Readers' Guide,* an audio-visual catalog, or the library in general, such a "discovery" exercise could become rather time-consuming and frustrating, however. In this case independent research is probably best as a culmination of inquiry teaching to evaluate student abilities to locate information, to separate the relevant from the irrelevant, and to use source materials effectively rather than as a learning experience.

Instead of having students flounder around in a library or devote excessive amounts of time to developing skills of library research to the exclusion of other skills, we can assemble useful data ourselves and present it to them via lecture, film, text, or some other media. Use of such media will thus enable students to practice other skills such as purposeful listening, viewing, or reading, asking questions, and so on. Or we might have the students use some of the techniques which social scientists use to collect evidence, including taking surveys, making field studies, developing and administering questionnaires, and conducting interviews. Engaging in these kinds of evidence-assembling activities will not only help students learn how to collect information but also suggest the attributes and limitations of these techniques. Such tasks ought to be special objectives of social studies instruction.

Finding and assembling evidence are only two of the skills important to hypothesis testing. There are many others which also must be used and taught. Thus, unless we deliberately wish to teach the skill of locating appropriate sources, we should provide the students with the needed sources and proceed to devise learning experiences in which they must draw the needed evidence from these sources. Such experiences should involve a whole host of special skills, for evidence is collected in a wide variety of ways—by reading or skimming written materials; by selective listening to audio presentations such as lectures, speeches, news broadcasts, conversations, debates, and the like; by reading maps, graphs, and pictures; and by observing personal experiences or real-life events. Evidence collecting might also involve designing and conducting surveys, interviews, and questionnaires. Students should have opportunities to practice all these techniques of gathering evidence.

It is important, therefore, that teachers select information contained in a wide variety of media for use in hypothesis testing. If, for example, the students are to continue their inquiry into whether or not certain peoples are Moslem, we may supply them with excerpts from a traveler's diary, some slides taken by an anthropologist, some recordings of their folklore, and perhaps some reproductions of their art or sculpture. We might even present in a lecture some data that may be otherwise unobtainable. In collecting data from these sources, the students will have an opportunity to practice or refine a larger number of skills than they could if working with only a single item such as a standard text.

Evaluation is also important to assembling evidence. As students search for and find data, they must determine which of their findings should be treated as evidence. Part of this decision is based on how closely related the data is to the hypothesis under consideration. But it is also based on the authenticity and accuracy of the data. Just because a piece of data is relevant to a hypothesis, it will not necessarily be useful in validating that hypothesis because it may be highly inaccurate, outdated, one-sided, or even a fraud. Consequently, students must learn to evaluate their evidence.

The teacher must design learning experiences in which students can examine data to distinguish statements of accepted fact from statements of opinion and to identify unstated assumptions, evidences of bias, and examples of faulty logic. They must determine the internal and external validity of the source itself—who created it, when and why, and what were his or their sources, biases, purposes? Students must also search for internal inconsistencies, for conclusions unsubstantiated by the evidence cited, and for card-stacking or emphasis on just one point of view. Such evaluation is as pertinent to work with maps, photographs, records, and filmstrips as it is to monographs, selections from diaries, newspapers, and documents.

Students should, for example, study how certain kinds of words, either written or spoken, convey meaning. The use of emotionally charged

words or words which connote value judgments reveals a great deal
about an author. They can give clues to the quality of his scholarship,
his biases, his assumptions, and even his intent. For instance, the following excerpt was purportedly written by a university professor:

> Before the arrival of Europeans, southeast Asia was a cultural
> wasteland. It had no history, no tradition of art or music, no
> civilization. Education, government, and religion were frustrated
> by the trivia of village life. Civilization could hardly thrive in
> crude thatched huts or behind the menacing masks of savage witch
> doctors. But the Europeans changed all this. Their guns brought
> law and order, the first requirement of civilization. Missionaries
> brought the blessings of Christianity and education and began the
> task of stamping out such barbarous practices as polygamy and
> semi-nudity. Traders introduced modern goods and acquainted
> the natives with the importance of money. Slothful natives were
> taught the virtues of hard work on European-owned plantations
> and railroad lines. Colonial governments instructed all people about
> democracy and how it works. In short, Europe shouldered the
> white man's burden and brought civilization to the primitive in-
> habitants of the jungles of southeast Asia.

Notice the evaluative words used by this author: "trivia," "crude,"
"modern," "savage," "blessings," and so on. Notice, too, the emotionally
charged words such as "menacing," "barbarous," "slothful," and "frus-
trated." These are important clues as to the frame of reference—the
biases and assumptions—of the author. There are also obvious statements of error—"It had no history. . . ."—and of opinion posing as
fact—". . . law and order, the first requirements of civilization." The
point of view of the author is made most clear in the way he has written.
Such an excerpt probably gives more of an insight into the society which
produced its author than into the subject it attempts to discuss. Practice
in analyzing newspaper articles, pictorial and audio materials, and textbooks in this fashion should be an integral part of hypothesis testing.
    Of course, students must also be given opportunities to evaluate the
content of the data. Is it an accurate portrayal of what it purports to
portray? Is it a primary account or a secondary account, and, if the
latter, on what is it based? These and other similar questions need to
be answered, and they can be by comparing sources of data. Students
can, for example, examine paragraphs on the same subject from a number of standard history texts, or they can be asked to evaluate excerpts
on the same topic from the works of a variety of scholars or to examine
and evaluate newspaper accounts, recollections of participants, and a
newsreel film of the same event. Evaluating data may be accomplished

in a variety of ways, but because it is an important skill in inquiring, it must be done.

Arranging Evidence

Meaningful analysis of evidence is as dependent on how that evidence is organized and displayed as it is on the quality of the data itself and on the frame of reference of the student. Hence, the next major step in testing a hypothesis is to prepare the assembled evidence for analysis. This preparation involves at least three distinct operations—translation, interpretation, and classification.

Before any information may be clearly comprehended, it must be in a form easily understood by the student. This frequently necessitates translating a piece of evidence into more familiar terms. Obviously translation would be required if the original evidence were written in a foreign language. But it is just as necessary in dealing with a highly technical piece of writing or even with something written in the idiom of sixteenth-century English or twentieth-century Mississippian. These too must be cast into the language of the student.

It is also important to translate evidence from one form into another. Pounds sterling need to be translated into dollars and cents when comparing them to dollars, for example. Kilometers need to be translated into miles, or vice versa, to make the units of measurement consistent. Moreover, evidence often should be translated into several different forms. The data for analyzing presidential election returns, for instance, would best be translated from a listing of which states voted for each candidate to a political map which might reveal areal relationships obscured by a mere alphabetical listing. And if that same data were displayed in another form, perhaps further relationships could be exposed.

Translating evidence from one form into another is important to preparing it for analysis because by so doing, recognition of new relationships may be made easier. Translation, however, is not the same as interpretation; caution must be exercised to prevent interpretation from coloring the results of the translation. Translation involves essentially displaying information originally presented in one form in another form. It requires students to "read" a graph or photograph for what it says and then to display this information in a new form. What the material literally "says" must not be tampered with, but it must be made crystal clear before it can take on any significant meaning.

To help students develop or use the skill of translating, the teacher might design activities in which they report in writing what they see in a slide or draw a map of a landscape pictured in a photograph or write in their own words the content of an ancient document. Such activities would be useful not only in preparing data for analysis but also in illustrating how translation can change the substance of something or how different people, because of their unique frames of reference, may translate the same items differently.

Suppose there is a photograph showing a large number of people moving among tables and counters overflowing with a variety of goods. Some people are handling some of these goods; others are giving something to persons stationed behind these tables; some of these people are, in turn, handing bundles or goods to those in the crowd, and so on. This is a literal translation into words of what a particular picture "says."

We might just as easily describe this picture as a market scene. But such a description would be interpretation, not translation. Interpretation is a skill quite distinct from that of reporting the literal contents of something. It involves making connections between what we see and what we already know—our own unique frame of reference and store of knowledge. Interpretation involves recasting or summarizing our perceptions in terms which describe or explain the interrelationships among them. Thus, interpreting this picture as a market scene neatly sums up its contents by giving them meaning.

Or, by way of another example, study the climograph in Figure 14.

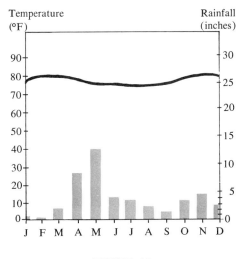

FIGURE 14

It says that the average rainfall for May for this particular station is about 13 inches, for September just under two inches, and for November almost five inches. It says further that the average annual rainfall here is about 49 inches. In addition, it says that the average daily

temperature in April is 80°F. These readings represent a literal translation of this data. However, the data might be interpreted to mean that
there seem to be two rainy periods—in April-May and again in
October-November—that the coolest period coincides with a period of
decreasing rainfall, and that the periods of highest average temperature
coincide with the periods of greatest rainfall.

Students need to realize the essential differences between translation
and interpretation, although both are important steps in arranging
evidence. Students must first ask or be asked: "What does the evidence
say?" or "What is going on here?" They must report literally what the
picture shows, the document says, the graph illustrates, and so on. Then
and only then should they ask, "What does it mean?" Only then may
they suggest the significance of what is going on or what the data means
to them. Every effort must be made to help students realize when they
are or should be translating and when they are or should be interpreting
because it is essential to avoid the confusion that will surely result should
these steps be unconsciously interchanged.

Another way of preparing evidence for analysis is to arrange it in
categories or classes. Classifying is especially important when dealing
with large masses of information. Categorizing individual pieces of information according to common characteristics facilitates the handling
of considerable amounts of data and also makes possible the detection
of a wide variety of interrelationships, trends, and sequences which otherwise might go unnoticed.

Students should be encouraged to categorize the same data in a
variety of ways. They should learn to group items according to ways of
arranging time—by centuries, by sequence, by cause and effect, and
within these by immediate and long-range. They should learn to group
data in terms of space—by relative position, by distance, by location,
and by association with other features. And they should also learn to
arrange data according to the factors which affect human life, such as
economic, political, social, intellectual, geographic, or religious.

Arranging data by ranking often involves personal opinions or preferences. Ranking certain events or features according to how good or
useful or right they may be for a certain person or group helps the student to clarify his own values and attitudes, for the way in which the
items are ranked may provide a good clue as to what he values or does
not value. Discussion of the reasons for a certain ranking is an important
technique in value clarification, but the ranking, or classifying, must take
place first.

Again, it is the teachers' task to help students learn to classify data.
At first this help may entail building deliberate exercises that require

the classification of certain data. Such exercises may consist of giving students certain items of data to place in prescribed categories, giving them lists of data to categorize however they wish, giving them data already categorized and having them describe the nature of the individual groups by developing appropriate descriptive titles for each, or having them search out their own data and group it as they see fit. Arranging data may be a class activity or a small group activity or an individual activity. Regardless of how it is carried out, however, it is a skill that should be mastered as part of inquiry teaching, for the ways in which evidence is arranged may facilitate or hinder its analysis.

Analyzing Evidence

Analysis is a very broad term. It is all too often used to suggest whatever it is that one does to test a hypothesis. It is more accurately used, however, to refer specifically to those mental operations involved in pulling evidence apart and refitting it in the search for new meaning. It does not refer to assembling or arranging evidence, but it does include the intellectual manipulation of data to identify similarities and differences, trends and sequences, regularities, and patterns of significance. Analysis cannot be done well until the data has been assembled and carefully arranged or displayed. It is an entirely separate operation, and a very sophisticated one at that.

Basically, analyzing evidence involves making inferences. Inferring is positing connections between the evidence and the hypothesis and among all the pieces of the evidence. It is going beyond the literal meaning of the evidence to new meaning.

What one looks for in analyzing any specific body of evidence depends, of course, on the nature of the evidence and the hypothesis under consideration. In general, however, an inquirer ought to seek out items that repeat themselves, cause and/or effect relationships, trends, sequences, patterns, regularities, and other kinds of interrelationships of significance. Knowing what to look for can be most helpful in suggesting where to look and how to go about it.

Analyzing data is a difficult task. It is made easier by careful but imaginative assembling and displaying of the evidence. An analysis of voting behavior will be facilitated, for instance, by displaying election returns, per capita income, and allotments for public works projects on maps of election districts and by using statistics showing registration and voting percentages, graphs of voting trends, and so on. Grouping this data according to political parties, nature of the elections, major campaign issues, events, or other categories may also help. But drawing inferences from this evidence—analyzing—is the culminating intellectual operation. It occurs in the mind of the student. The results of another's analysis may be communicated to him, but this is no substitute for his own analysis. *Finding meaning in data is the essence of learning, and analysis is where it occurs.*

This phase of inquiring may be built around a host of questions, including:

> What does this evidence mean?
>
> How is it related to another piece of evidence?
>
> Which piece of evidence came first?
>
> What is the relationship between this evidence and the hypothesis?

Regardless of who asks the questions, student or teacher, it is important in this phase of inquiring that students refer periodically to the hypothesis being tested in order to avoid being sidetracked. Periodic reviews or summaries of the extent to which the evidence thus far examined supports or refutes the hypothesis are also worthwhile. Important, too, is recognition of the tentative nature of the hypothesis and of the very real possibility that it might be invalidated by this analysis. These are, of course, student-centered tasks, but the teacher can guide them via oral questioning or written study guides or even by the way in which he structures the materials.

There are two tools important to the conduct of hypothesis testing. One is questioning. The other is data.

Data is used throughout this stage of learning. When first using an inquiry-teaching strategy, it is often desirable to provide the students with all the needed data so as to maximize the time available for working with it. Sometimes we need provide only data relevant to the hypothesis. But as the students become more competent in inquiring, data unrelated to the hypothesis should also be presented so that students may practice the skills of separating the relevant from the irrelevant.

Examining all known data relevant to a particular hypothesis, although desirable, is not usually possible or practical. Students, therefore, must become accustomed to arriving at conclusions on the basis of somewhat incomplete or suspect evidence. At the same time they must know that because their evidence is incomplete, their conclusions must be at best tentative until confirmed or modified in the light of later experience with additional data.

Under no circumstances should the data made available to the students be biased one way or another. Evidence contradictory to the hypothesis must not be suppressed or ignored. As the experts in the content field, we are responsible for ensuring that this does not happen, that data representative of all views on a hypothesis is examined.

Questioning is also an important tool in this stage of inquiry teaching.[9] Whether teacher or student initiated, written or oral, the general kinds of questions that must be asked in order to direct students to the appropriate intellectual operations are:

1. If your hypothesis is true, then what kinds of evidence do you expect to find? If your hypothesis is true, then what kinds of evidence do you not expect to find?
    Identifying Needed Evidence

2. Where will you find it? How?
    Collecting Evidence

3. Is the evidence authentic? Is it valid? Is it reliable?
    Evaluating Evidence

4. What does it say?
    Translating Evidence

5. What does it mean?
    Interpreting Evidence

6. How can it be classified?
    Classifying Evidence

7. Why did you classify it as you did?
    Seeking Relationships

8. How is this similar to other evidence? How do they differ?
    Noting Similarities and Differences

9. Which comes first? Which is nearest? Which repeat?
    Identifying Trends, Sequences, and Regularities

10. What does all this evidence do to our hypothesis?

---

[9] Several different ways of classifying questions have been devised. See, for example: Ronald Lippitt et al., *The Teacher's Role in Social Science Investigation* (Chicago: Science Research Associates, 1969), p. 19; and Norris M. Sanders, *Classroom Questions: What Kinds?* (New York: Harper & Row, 1966). This latter volume is a valuable source of model questions for use in stimulating all types of intellectual activity and should be referred to frequently in planning inquiry teaching.

In sum, hypothesis testing means students must assemble, arrange, and analyze evidence. Whether students are clarifying values or testing alternative solutions, hypothetical answers, or plans of attack, these are the operations in which they engage. It is here that new learning occurs.

Developing
a Conclusion

Inquiry usually moves toward a conclusion. Concluding consists primarily of refitting the evidence in such a way that it takes on meaning relevant to the hypothesis being tested. This combining of parts into a whole is often referred to as synthesizing. It involves the same kind of mental operation used in formulating a hypothesis. But a hypothesis represents only a possible explanation because it is based on only fragmentary evidence and often developed without any deliberate analysis of an almost conclusive amount of evidence.

A conclusion is usually a statement about the validity of the original hypothesis. It is really a judgment about the rightness or wrongness of the hypothesis. It may be merely a reaffirmation of this guess, but more often than not, it is an elaboration with certain qualifications or even substantial modifications. Regardless of which form a conclusion takes, however, and because it is built on specific but often limited evidence, it is still rather restricted in scope or applicability. If a concept, it is usually ill-defined. If a statement relating various facts or concepts, it is generally limited by specific referents in time and place. Conclusions that result from this stage of inquiry must still be subject to considerable qualification and modification as new data are later brought to bear on them.

Testing a hypothesis may cast serious doubts on its validity if not invalidate it altogether. In this case the student learns that his "answer" is wrong—the evidence does not support it. Such a result does not mean, however, that the whole effort has been wasted. "Wrong answers" are not useless answers. On the contrary, a hypothesis that has not been substantiated indicates a line of probing that need not be pursued further and thus eliminates a whole collection of data that need not be looked into any deeper. In this sense invalid hypotheses play a positive role in learning.

In guiding the development of conclusions, the teacher must direct students into learning experiences that require them to combine identified relationships among the evidence and between the evidence and hypothesis into statements that bear on the initial problem. Students must be asked to state explicitly the relationship between this rearranged evidence and the hypothesis being investigated. If the results invalidate the hypothesis, the student must return to the original question, develop a new hypothesis, and proceed again to test it. This repetition is, in fact, the way in which most problems are resolved. By repeated hypothesizing and testing, progress is made towards a valid conclusion. If, on the other hand, the conclusion affirms or modifies the original hypothesis or suggests an acceptable solution or answer to the original problem, it may be accepted as at least a temporary valid culmination of the investigation.

The utility and even validity of conclusions drawn as a result of this process depend, of course, upon the amount and validity of the evidence on which they are based. A hypothesis, which in itself is a kind of conclusion, is very suspect because it is based on limited evidence. A conclusion built on a test against more evidence may be only slightly more substantial, for it cannot be accepted as absolutely final or true until it is tested against all relevant data. In many cases this is impossible. Yet, such testing may very well be an ultimate objective of inquiry teaching.

Applying the Conclusion to New Data

At first glance, drawing a conclusion may represent a perfectly logical final step in inquiry—the problem is resolved or the question answered. And this may be so. But making one's own conclusion does not represent a psychologically satisfying final step. For most people, one question still remains: "How do I know that the conclusion I have drawn is really the right one?" This nagging question compels us to go one step further—to apply our conclusion to new data to see if what we think is true really is true. Hence the final step in inquiry and inquiry teaching—applying the conclusion to new data.

This final step serves several purposes. It brings psychological as well as substantive closure to an otherwise still unsettled situation. It permits the inquirer to find out if his own independent inquiry is indeed substantiated by other sources. This step also frequently expands the original conclusion. Applying a conclusion to new but related evidence may well make that conclusion less specific, more applicable to or explanative of the class of data to which it is related without being tied to any specific set of that data. Thus, the conclusion becomes more general, more conceptual. Generalizing and conceptualizing represent for many the final, most advanced stage of thinking. It thus must be considered as a culminating step in any strategy of inquiry teaching.

Generalizing requires that a conclusion derived from examining a specific set of evidence be treated as a hypothesis for testing against new evidence. This means that the inquirer must repeat the same kinds of operations that led to his conclusion in the first place. He must assemble, arrange, and analyze new evidence relating to this conclusion and then determine the extent to which his original conclusion explains this evidence or is substantiated by it. Such an operation may substantially modify his original conclusion. But going through this process is just as likely not to change it markedly. Instead, applying a conclusion to new data, if the conclusion is substantiated, grounds the conclusion in more evidence—it gives the original conclusion greater validity because now the conclusion is based on more evidence and has withstood the test of more examples. The result is a much more reliable piece of knowledge.

Applying a conclusion to new data involves checking the conclusion against data relating to it but as yet unused by the inquirer. This data may be the findings of recognized experts who have made inquiries into the same or different but related evidence. It may be the "concluding essay" which generally sums up the major established points relating to the problem at hand (but which all too often serves only to tell the inquirer what he should have discovered through his own inquiry). This new data may even be the opinions or conclusions reached by his peers who have also gone through the same inquiry.

These types of data are quite commonly used in inquiry teaching today. But accurate or timesaving as they may be, they have serious drawbacks. For one thing, checking what the others in class think about something can easily degenerate into voting on the accuracy of knowledge—"How many agree with Susan? Only ten out of twenty-five? Well, Susan, I guess you're wrong!"—an indefensible approach to learning and teaching. Moreover, checking one's conclusion against what the experts say (and what makes an expert an expert?) or against what the textbook author wrote in his chapter summary might be considered a cop-out. Inquiring is hard work. As soon as students find that such expert opinions are available for use or that such chapter summaries do exist, they are likely to feel that further inquiry on their own is a waste of time. "Why should I go through all that work to solve a problem or discover something when I can find the answer at the end of the chapter?" As invalid as this reasoning may be from the teacher's point of view, it is a very real factor in the attitudes of many students toward thinking in the classroom.

If students must use what the experts say to check their conclusions, and this can sometimes be done very effectively, they should not treat them as having the answer but as being just additional sources of data. Students should treat their own conclusions as valid and then use them to check the accuracy of the opinions of experts and the evidence they cite in support of these opinions. A chapter summary ought to be treated merely as more data, not as answers but as mere opinions. Then the students can check the accuracy of the statements in this summary against what they have already found out. Certainly all kinds of new questions will arise in the process, and the student conclusions arrived at earlier will be modified and treated with some suspicion. And the opinions of the experts and textbook author may also be received with skepticism. Students should question what the so-called expert and the chapter summary say rather than what they themselves have concluded, if such a conclusion has been based on reasoned inquiry.

The most effective, but also most time-consuming, type of data against which to apply a conclusion is data which is relevant to the conclusion but which was not used in developing that conclusion. The inquirer should use his conclusion to make sense of this new evidence. If the conclusion does this satisfactorily, then the chances of its being valid are greater than they were before this stage of inquiring. If the conclusion does not account for or make sense of this new data, then it will surely require some modification.

For example, suppose that students have concluded after studying information about the War of 1812, the Mexican War, the Spanish-American War, and the Spanish Civil War that the major causes of wars are economic. Of all the possible wars they could have studied, they have only studied four. Their conclusion is quite limited in scope. If they want this conclusion to explain the cause of all wars, they must treat it as a hypothesis and submit it to the test of information about other wars, such as the War of the Roses, World War I, the Napoleonic Wars, the Sino-Japanese War, the Boer War, and others. Then the conclusions they arrive at as a result of this investigation will be less tied to a specific country or time or place. They will be much more general, more applicable to a wider variety of data that still has the same essential characteristics.

Applying a conclusion to new data may result in different levels or types of knowledge. Concepts, or mental images, evolve in this way. Value preferences and clarification of personal value systems also evolve through this step of inquiry. So, too, do generalizations. Since generalizations are sometimes considered to be the ultimate goal of much social studies teaching, a further word should be said about them here.

A generalization is a statement of relationship between several concepts. As defined by Bertha Davis, it is a true statement which has no specific referent in time or place.[10] That is, a generalization is a statement which is generally true for the entire class of things to which it refers, regardless of where or when they exist. For example, if the following statements can be considered true, they may be considered generalizations:

All American presidents have been men.

Wars are caused primarily for economic reasons.

A people's way of life is shaped by both its habitat and its level of technology.

Each of these statements describes a relationship between two or more distinct categories or concepts. The first describes a relationship between *presidents* and *men*. It applies to all presidents. The second describes a relationship between *wars* and *economic reasons*—regardless of time or place. And the third example describes a relationship between a people's *way of life* on the one hand and both *habitat* and *level of technology* on the other.

Generalizations are end products of learning. They serve many purposes, one of which is helping to predict or explain possible relationships between similar categories of things whenever they may be encountered in the future. Generalizations also serve as a handy way of summarizing what is thought to be true about all similar categories or factors even though these may never have been directly observed or tested. Thus, knowing the generalization that "All American presidents have been men" will enable a student to predict at least one characteristic of future presidents. It may also enable him to sift through a random list of names and discard all women's names as he tries to determine just precisely who some past presidents have been. The great value of a generalization is its utility in predicting about a variety of similar situations.

Generalizations are not by any means absolute truths. The degree to which they approximate reality depends considerably upon the amount of data which has been studied in developing them. Generalizations are at best statements that may be considered relatively true for operational purposes only, but are still held as tentative. All generalizations fairly beg for modification (as the "exception which proves the

---

[10] Bertha Davis, "Conceptual Teaching in the Social Studies," in *New Approaches to the Teaching of Social Studies: A Report of the Eleventh Yale Conference on the Teaching of Social Studies, April 15 and 16* (New Haven: Yale University Office of Teacher Training, 1966), pp. 48–51.

rule"). Part of the value system of inquiry is the rejection of absolutes, and generalizations are not exempt.

Generalizations should not be confused with understandings. Understandings are less sweeping than generalizations in that they refer specifically to some time, place, or thing. Yet understandings, like generalizations, describe a relationship between two or more concepts. The following may be considered examples of understandings:

> President Abraham Lincoln was a man.
>
> The Spanish-American War was caused primarily by economic factors.
>
> The way of life of the !Kung is shaped by both their harsh habitat and their simple technology.

Understandings, like generalizations, represent a product of learning, but they do not result from the final step of inquiring. Instead, understandings may be equated with the statements developed as conclusions in the preceding or fourth step of inquiry teaching. A statement that evolves from testing a hypothesis may be described as an understanding because it customarily describes a rather precise relationship between two very specific factors and because it has specific referents in time and/or place. Understandings thus have little predictive value. Nevertheless, understandings often serve as the building blocks for higher cognitive knowledge.

Generalizations evolve from understandings. If we have come to know that most American presidents were men, then we can generalize about all American presidents and state, "All American presidents have been men." If we investigate a specific war and conclude that it was caused primarily for economic reasons and if we then investigate another war and yet another and another, reaching the same conclusion (understanding) each time, we can soon generalize about the causes of wars: "Wars are caused primarily for economic reasons." Specific understandings on related topics may evolve into single, more broadly applicable generalizations.

Applying a conclusion, whether it be in the form of an understanding, concept, or other type of knowledge, to new data is the final step in inquiry teaching. This step enables the student to complete his inquiry by giving it conceptual meaning, and it also helps to satisfy his natural desire to know if he is correct in his conclusions. Since most students do not know how to engage effectively in this step of inquiring, they need extensive teacher guidance at first. In time, however, they can be expected to apply their conclusions to new data on their own, in independent-study learning situations. Regardless of how this fifth step is organized, it is crucial to effective inquiry teaching.

Summary

Inquiry teaching is based directly on how we learn by inquiring. This strategy requires teachers to create learning experiences in which students must identify problems for investigation, invent hypotheses relative to these problems, test these hypotheses against evidence, draw conclusions about the validity of these hypotheses, and finally, either devise new hypotheses for testing or apply these conclusions to new data. This teaching strategy can serve as the basis of daily lessons, weekly units of instruction, one-year courses, and even entire K–12 curricula. Inquiry teaching is a conceptual structure for teaching and learning that develops thinking skills and their associated cognitive and affective dimensions to their fullest potentials. Accomplishing these objectives is considered a primary task of social studies teaching today.

Inquiry Teaching in Action	**5**

A strategy of inquiry teaching is complex indeed. Yet this complexity does not mean that inquiry teaching is unworkable in a classroom setting. Inquiry teaching may be as simple or sophisticated as a teacher wishes to make it. But whatever the degree to which he utilizes this strategy, the resultant learning experiences must be built around at least the four basic steps of *problem, hypothesis, test,* and *conclusion.*

An Inquiry
Lesson

How does a lesson built on an inquiry-teaching strategy proceed? The short investigation of the Asante which launches Chapter 1 is built on an inquiry-teaching strategy. If you, attempted to work through it as directed by the questions, then you were engaging in an inquiry lesson. If you did not, turn back to page 1 and go through the lesson. Then reflect on what you did in terms of the model of inquiry teaching described in the preceding pages.

Here is another lesson, structured just like the Asante lesson but in much greater detail. As you read through this lesson, try to keep in mind the basic steps of our model of

inquiry teaching and compare what you do here with what you did with
the Asante. This new lesson has been used with students and teachers of
all ability levels in social studies classes from grades 4-12. What is presented here represents a composite of how this lesson generally develops
with all these groups. This is not a script. Instead, it is a descriptive
narrative that invites you, the reader, to become involved as if you were
actually participating in the lesson as a student.

Suppose we are studying, in a world cultures class, different cultural
regions of the "non-Western" world in an attempt to develop certain
generalizations and concepts about human beings and their behavior as
well as to develop certain intellectual and other skills. And suppose
further that we are currently involved in a study of Africa, trying to
learn more about the various peoples who inhabit this part of our
world. We could approach this study of Africa by examining in some
detail a number of different peoples who live there. One people we
might study, for example, are the Hausa.

Problem. . . . There are probably few of us who know anything at
all about the Hausa. Consequently one way to initiate our study might
be to examine some specific data relative to the Hausa and use that
as the take-off point for hypothesizing. The question, or problem, then
could be *What are the Hausa like?* What follows is a list of Hausa
words with their English meanings as excerpted from a standard Hausa-
English dictionary. These words are commonly spoken in everyday
Hausa life. Examination of them may provide some useful clues as to
what the Hausa are like. Examine these words and decide what seem
to be at least three major characteristics of the Hausa or their culture:

SELECTED HAUSA WORDS[11]

HAUSA	ENGLISH	HAUSA	ENGLISH
auduga	cotton	bara	servant
akwiya	goat	bashi	to owe
albasa	onion	bauta	slavery
aljumma'a	Sabbath, Friday	birni	walled town, city
Allah	God	bukka	tent
alwashi	agreement	cukumara	cheese
araha	cheap	da	son

---

[11] I am indebted to Professor Anthony Kirk-Greene of St. Anthony's College,
Oxford, for assistance in preparing this list.

HAUSA	ENGLISH	HAUSA	ENGLISH
daki	house	mai-fito	tax collector
damuna	rainy season	makeri	blacksmith
dan kasuwa	trader, market man	mallam	teacher, learned man
dawa	desert	manshanu	butter
doka	a prohibition, law	rakumi	camel
doki	horse	rani	dry season
doya	yams	saniya	cow
falke	merchant	sayewa	to sell
fatalwa	ghost	shirigi jirgi	canoe
fito	tax	tanderu	furnace, clay oven
gaci	brass, copper		
gardi	schoolmaster	tshimua	mosque
gishiri	salt	tsatsa	to rust
gonah	farm	tsauni	mountain
hanya	road	tunkiya	sheep
kafirci	witchcraft	uwa	mother
kakata	grandmother	wali	prophet
kamu kifi	to catch fish	wa	brother
kanuwar ubana	aunt	wanakiri	devil
kidaya	account	yi addu'a	to pray
leima	umbrella	zinaria	gold
littafi	*Koran,* book	zorah	bargain
mai-aski	barber	zunufi	sin
mai-bashi	debtor		

. . . *Hypothesis.* . . . What characteristics did you infer? List them here:

The Hausa certainly seem to be a religious people. They have words for all the things we usually associate with religious behavior—sin, pray, God, sabbath, and devil. In fact, it appears that they may even be Moslem. The use of the word Allah for God and words for *Koran,* mosque, and prophet certainly suggest this. So, too, does the fact that the Hausa word *aljumma'a* means Friday as well as Sabbath, and Friday is the Moslem Sabbath. So perhaps the Hausa are Moslem.

Or maybe they practice witchcraft! There is a word meaning witchcraft as well as words for ghost and devil. It could be that some Hausa have been converted to Islam while others still practice a more traditional religion. Perhaps two different religions exist side by side, or perhaps the Hausa practice two religions simultaneously.

The Hausa may also be farmers. There are many words that suggest this. Different types of domesticated farm animals are mentioned including sheep, goat, horse, and cow. There are words for farm and and for products commonly associated with agricultural pursuits. In addition, the word for rainy season suggests a climate suitable for farming.

There may be some type of well-organized government in Hausaland, too. There evidently are laws, but whether they are religious or political is not clear. But laws imply a lawmaker, whether it be an individual or group of individuals. The presence of a word for taxes implies that there is someone to levy taxes. There appears also to be a tax collector as well as a schoolmaster. These words suggest a rather formalized governmental structure, one which employs a number of people, each responsible for a certain specialized task designed to serve the group rather than an individual.

Perhaps the Hausa live in a region where the climate varies. There is a word for desert, but they probably don't live there because the words for fishing and canoe suggest the presence of some river or lake in the region. There is also a word for mountains, so perhaps they live between the desert and the mountains. That there are words for rainy season and dry season may mean that the area which the Hausa inhabit is a semiarid grassland with sharp seasonal variations in rainfall and temperature.

The Hausa may also be traders. They have words for agreement, cheap, bargain, account, debtor, and sell. They seem to have a number of handcrafted or manufactured goods, including brass and umbrellas, as well as certain agricultural products that are typically found in market-oriented economies. Apparently they engage in all the activities associated with trading including bookkeeping and buying and selling on credit. Their economy may be highly commercial.

There are other inferences that we can make about the Hausa on the basis of a study of these words. Some words here, for example, suggest that the Hausa may be nomads (tent, camel), that they have an extended family structure (grandmother, aunt), that they engage in fishing (canoe, to catch fish), and that they have an economy built on specialization of labor because they not only farm and trade but also have skilled craftsmen (blacksmith, barber) who specialize in the production of different types of goods and services.

However, let us stop at this point and review what we have said about the Hausa. We have listed a number of possible characteristics of these people. The Hausa, we think:

are Moslem
believe in witchcraft
are farmers
have a well-organized government
live in a semiarid grassland
are traders
are nomads
have an extended family system
engage in fishing
have specialization of labor
are skilled craftsmen

Add whatever other characteristics you infer about the Hausa to the above list.

. . . *Test.* . . . Now, how do we know we are correct? What can we do to check the accuracy of the preceding guesses? There are any number of sources to which we can turn for help. We may, for example, check what the text has to say about Africa, Africans, or the Hausa. Or, we can go to the library and look up these same subjects in an encyclopedia or other specialized books on Africa or African peoples—or with luck, on the Hausa—that might help us. We might also look through the *Readers' Guide* for articles in periodicals such as the *National Geographic Magazine* or some similar publication. Even a newspaper or news magazine might contain some information on the Hausa.

We might also consult the human resource. Perhaps there are some people in our community who know something about Africa in general or the Hausa in particular. A returned missionary may now be serving in a local church; a returned Peace Corps volunteer or soldier or government official (such as an employee of the Agency for International Development or the State Department) might also live in the community. Perhaps some students or local families have recently toured Africa, or maybe a local teacher or student spent some months there in study, in travel, or in an exchange program. A professor in a local college or university may be a specialist on the Hausa or on some subject such as anthropology. Of course, personnel in the embassy of the country in which the Hausa live may also help just as might African students studying in this country. With luck, a Hausa might be studying at a local college and consent to visit our class.

We might use audio and visual media. An enormous number of films, film loops, filmstrips, slide sets, picture cards, programs, tapes, and records about Africa are available. Some of these might contain information about the Hausa. If we could identify and locate these materials, we might be able to check the accuracy of our guesses.

We do, in fact, have some photographic information about the Hausa. Examining it may help us determine the extent to which the hypotheses we have made are correct. But before doing so, we must identify the kinds of evidence we wish to find—or not find—if our hypotheses are valid. That is, we need to ask ourselves, "If our hypotheses are correct, then what specific evidence should we expect to see?" And conversely, we need to ask, "If our hypotheses are correct, then what evidence do we not want to find?"

For example, if the Hausa really are Moslem, then what should we see in any representative sampling of pictures to prove they are Moslem? Perhaps we want to see a mosque—a building with that peculiarly shaped dome and tall towers or minarets. It would help, too, if we saw people in public prayer, praying in the traditional Moslem style; if we saw veiled women (what little we know about Islam tells us Moslem women are veiled, although some in our class might insist this is no longer true); if inside a Hausa home we saw a copy of the *Koran;* if we saw men wearing the small cap traditionally worn by Moslem men. If in studying these pictures we find such evidence, then we can feel somewhat sure that our guess that the Hausa are Moslem is correct. If we fail to see any Christian churches or Jewish synagogues, Buddhist shrines or Hindu temples, and if we fail to see widespread use of the *Torah, Bible,* or writings of Confucius, then we might even be more convinced than ever that we are right.

Let us examine another hypothesis. What do we want to see in the pictures if the Hausa really believe in witchcraft? A witchdoctor? What does a witchdoctor look like? A doctor in our society often wears a certain type of costume when performing his duties and sometimes "decorates" himself with certain distinguishing objects. Does a witchdoctor do the same? What little we know about African witchdoctors, or any other witchdoctors for that matter, suggests that they too, when performing their rituals, wear certain types of costumes—face masks, grass skirts, and colored sashes perhaps. They also decorate themselves, not with stethoscopes, tongue depressors, and prescription tablets, but with rattles, beads, gongs, and other tools of their trade. Our doctors dispense pills and shots; witchdoctors dispense potions and incense. Both often talk (and sometimes write) in unintelligible tongues. Perhaps if we saw a number of Africans who fit this image of a witchdoctor, we might be correct in saying that some Hausa do indeed practice witchcraft.

What about farmers? If the Hausa really are farmers, then what do we expect to see? Farms? What distinguishes a farm from a suburban or city home? Cultivated fields? Farm buildings—barns, sheds, and the like? Farm tools—hoes, plows, reapers? People engaged in farming— harvesting, planting, plowing, milking, and so on? Farm animals—cows, goats, and sheep? Pigs (if they are Moslem)? Farm products, perhaps in storage or in a market place? If we see these things in a series of pictures, then perhaps the Hausa are farmers. And if we fail to see anything indicative of extensive nonagricultural pursuits—such as tent villages, roving herds of animals, numerous factories or mines—then perhaps the Hausa really are farmers.

What about the well-organized government we hypothesized? What do we want to see that will convince us the Hausa do in fact have a well-organized as opposed to a "primitive" government? A tax collector? How will we recognize him when we see him? Government buildings? What distinguishes them from other buildings? What physical evidence is illustrative of such a governmental system? Street signs? Uniformed men such as army officers or police? School buildings? A post office building? Law courts or legislative chambers? If the Hausa really do have a well-organized government, then are these the things we expect to see? If the Hausa really do have a well-organized government, then what is it we don't want to see?

This question, "If the Hausa are _____, then I expect to see _____." (and where possible, "If the Hausa are _____, then I don't expect to see _____."), must be asked for each hypothesis formulated about the Hausa before examining—indeed, before even collecting—any evidence. Once we have listed the kinds of evidence needed to prove our guesses valid, we can begin working with the information on the Hausa that is available to us.

The photographs on the following pages were taken in Hausaland within the past several years. Study them. What do they show? To what extent does the information contained in these photographs validate or invalidate our hypotheses about the Hausa (as stated on page 93)? Select one of these hypotheses, determine what kinds of evidence you wish to find, or not find, if the hypothesis is correct, and examine each of the following photographs to see if you can find that evidence. Then note in your head or in the margin next to that hypothesis what evidence you find. Follow this same procedure for each hypothesis you test.

1   (Courtesy of David Allyn)

2   (Courtesy of Anthony Kirk-Greene)

3 (Courtesy of Anthony Kirk-Greene)

4 (Courtesy of Anthony Kirk-Greene)

5   (Courtesy of David Allyn)

6   (Courtesy of Schneider's of Athens)

7   (Courtesy of David Allyn)

8   (Courtesy of Schneider's of Athens)

Are the Hausa Moslem? What evidence do you find that bears on this hypothesis? Do you see some of the things we expected to see which indicate that the Hausa really are Moslem? Certainly the photograph of the people bowed in public prayer in front of the mosque suggests that at least some Hausa are Moslem. Is there any evidence in any of the other photographs to either substantiate or contradict this conclusion? What about the clothing worn by the people in photographs 1, 3, 5, 6 and 8? How does this evidence affect our hypothesis?

Do the Hausa believe in or practice witchcraft? Did you find in these photographs any of the things we identified as evidence that this hypothesis is valid? What is it? Do the Hausa, or at least some of them, believe in witchcraft?

To what extent are these and our other hypotheses valid, at least in terms of the evidence we have thus far examined? Are the Hausa craftsmen? Nomads? Farmers? Do they have specialization of labor, a well-organized government, an extended family system? Examine the evidence you have collected for each hypothesis. Does it relate to that hypothesis? Does it substantiate it or invalidate it? What, then, is the fate of each hypothesis? Indicate (perhaps by circling) those hypotheses which you think are probably true for at least most Hausa; indicate (perhaps with a check) those hypotheses which do not appear valid in terms of this evidence; and indicate (with a question mark) those about which we can make no decision because there is little or no evidence here relative to them.

And what about new ideas? Is there anything in these pictures that suggests features of Hausa life or culture which we have not mentioned before? Does it appear that there is a definite class structure, for example? In photograph 1 there is obviously a person of some importance riding in a position of honor. People seem to be paying him respect. In the dictionary list, moreover, there were words for slave and servant. Do these bits of evidence suggest a feature we may have so far omitted? Add it to our list of hypotheses. What other possible characteristics of the Hausa can be added as well?

. . . and Conclude. At this point, what do we know about the Hausa? Or better yet, what can we say with some degree of certainty about at least some Hausa? Can we make a statement that says something like "Based on the evidence examined here, at least some Hausa appear to be Moslem, some are farmers . . ."? What else would you add to this statement? Write out a complete statement, being as specific as pos-

sible, which summarizes at this point, what may be true about the Hausa:

Perhaps we can agree that the Hausa are a varied lot—some are Moslem, some are farmers, some are traders, and some are craftsmen. Yet there is a distinct possibility that one individual may fill several of these roles simultaneously. Some Hausa live a rural existence, but others seem to be urban dwellers. The Hausa have an apparently sophisticated governmental system with traces of a rather stratified social structure. Their society seems to be male-centered, at least from the evidence thus far examined.

But what next? Some of our hypotheses appear to be valid. Others do not. Still others are untested by this evidence. Moreover, our list of hypotheses has perhaps grown. On the basis of our examination of the available evidence we may have hypothesized several additional features of Hausa life which we had not thought of before. What can we do now to test our new hypotheses, to test further those we think are accurate, and to determine the fate of those we wish to discard or those about which we are, at present, still uncertain?

Additional evidence is needed. Perhaps we can find some books on the Hausa in the library. An atlas, for example, might show us where they live. Then we could search out information on that particular country or countries. We might even write to the appropriate embassies to seek help in the form of printed information, films, or perhaps even a tape-recorded response to questions taped and sent to them for their reactions. Perhaps a search of audio-visual catalogs will reveal other useful materials as well.

Regardless of what sources we consult, however, it is clear that we need much more evidence before we can consider any of our hypotheses valid or invalid. We must continue testing them against new evidence yet to be collected. Then and only then will we be able to make statements about the Hausa with any reasonable assurance that we are correct. And, of course, being human—just like the scholar on the train to Mamaresch—we will probably sooner or later seek some authoritative sources which describe the salient features of the Hausa and their culture. We can check our entire investigation against these sources and finally know for sure whether or not our conclusions correspond with those of recognized experts.

The Lesson in
Retrospect

Let us stop and review what we have been doing. We have been going through a learning experience built directly on an inquiry-teaching strategy. We started with a problem—What are the Hausa like? Next we hypothesized some answers to this problem. Then we tested these hypotheses against information about the Hausa. Finally we made decisions about the validity of our hypotheses—we drew conclusions about our investigation. In some instances we found our hypotheses to be at least partially valid; in other instances hypotheses were invalidated or even untested by the information we used. Some new hypotheses may have emerged as well. At any rate, we finally concluded something—if ever so little and ever so tentative—about what the Hausa are like.

Our investigation started with the problem, "What are the Hausa like?" In actual practice, this problem is student initiated and grows out of a sequence of prior learning experiences. Here, however, for demonstration purposes, it is already given. Consequently, this particular problem is really a teacher problem. This demonstration lesson relies on the desire of the learners to participate in the demonstration and to motivate sufficiently the subsequent investigation. In an actual classroom learning experience however, a teacher-initiated problem may not always lead to the most productive learning. In order for the most effective inquiry to occur, the students must perceive a problem which they feel is worthy of further investigation.

This initiatory problem appears at first to be a simple one, but it is actually quite complex. Making it meaningful and manageable requires that it be broken down into a number of smaller, workable problems. Thus, instead of a scatter-gun approach at the start, each student should search for only three or four characteristics of the Hausa. Then, having secured as many different ideas as possible, the class can proceed to examine each characteristic individually. In testing each hypothesized characteristic, we are asking in effect, "Are the Hausa whatever it is we think they are?" Here we are actually reducing our initial but general problem to a number of very specific questions, the answers to which will help us develop an answer to the overall problem.

Hypothesizing answers to a problem may be done in many ways. We can, for example, base this activity entirely on whatever the learner can recall about the subject at hand. Most of us know something about Africans—erroneous or vague as that something may be. If someone were to ask what we think the Hausa are like, we might very well respond, on the basis of how we imagine Africans, that the Hausa are simple farmers who live a rural existence, wear few clothes, worship pagan gods, and are, in a word, rather "primitive" black people. Such would be one way to launch this study.

However, in this demonstration the learners are to hypothesize on the basis of more direct input, on the basis of some common data provided by the teacher. This input not only gives the students practice and guidance in developing the skill of making inferences from new data but also allows the teacher to determine to some extent the kinds of hypotheses that may result so that the data necessary to test these hypotheses may be made available. Otherwise valuable time may be lost in a search that very well may fail to turn up the needed data (given the limits of the school library and other available resources) and thus deflate whatever student interest has been aroused. Serious frustration may result on the part of all concerned.

Thus, the learners were supplied with some data on the Hausa as the basis for their hypothesizing. Yet in spite of the fact that all had the same data and presumably the same amount of prior knowledge about the Hausa, a wide variety of different hypotheses were suggested. Why? Because each learner has a unique background of experience—a frame of reference or a set of concepts—that directs his attention to different aspects of new experience and leads him to ask different kinds of questions of it. What one person sees in any body of data may legitimately be quite different from what another sees because each of us tends to ask different questions of that data. Hence, even though the data input in this activity strives to establish a common ground for the activity, the unique backgrounds of the students bring forth the divergent thinking characteristic of genuine hypothesizing. What appears at first to be a highly directed activity is, in reality, very much learner directed and individualized.

The same observation may be made of the testing phase of this lesson. All learners have identical information to examine. Yet a wide variety of different conclusions may be reached, again depending on the previous experience and talents of each individual learner. This time, however, because we have been testing the same hypotheses, there can emerge a core of "answers" on which all can agree—not because one answer is inherently correct and another inherently incorrect but because proper use of the process and skills of hypothesis testing with due awareness of the limitations thereof can only result logically in certain positions regarding the hypothesis under examination. Practicing and refining these skills are important objectives of such a learning experience.

There are many separate skills and steps involved in hypothesis testing. After identifying the kinds of evidence needed to substantiate the hypotheses, the students need to collect information that may contain this evidence. In this particular lesson, this information is supplied by the teacher through pure exposition. This same information might be presented to the students by a lecture, filmstrip, speaker, sound film, recording, or book. Furnishing information is perfectly legitimate if the learners then use it as a reservoir from which to draw information (evidence) relevant to their hypotheses. It is also legitimate if an objective of the lesson is not to teach students how to locate information but rather how to read, interpret, and analyze this information.

Learners cannot be expected to devote equal attention to practicing each inquiry skill in every learning experience because the lesson will become so drawn out that its whole purpose will be forgotten before closure is achieved. Learning is much more fun and productive in terms of knowledge and skills learned if different lessons single out one or two skill and knowledge objectives on which to focus. The key is to have successive lessons concentrate on different objectives instead of repeating the same ones over and over.

Once the information is obtained, it should be evaluated. Note that in this particular instance, however, the data used seems to have been accepted as authentic. It's validity was not questioned at all. The authority of the teacher or source was evidently sufficient to guarantee the authenticity of the data. Again, while learning how to evaluate data may be an important objective of inquiry teaching, it is neither necessary nor desirable to emphasize this skill every single time we engage in inquiry, for such emphasis may serve only to detract from other, relatively more important learning objectives for this particular lesson. Experience leads us to accept as accurate and reliable many sources to which we can refer without detailed evaluation each time we use them. It is as important for students to learn when to evaluate information and its sources as well as how to evaluate such material.

Arranging evidence for analysis usually follows the identification, collection, and evaluation of data. In this particular lesson these skills are used in reading the photographs—in trying to determine what they show, in interpreting their content in terms of the kinds of evidence we are seeking, and in grouping selected bits of evidence according to the specific hypothesis to which they are related.

The actual validation or invalidation of the hypotheses results from noting relationships among certain evidence—such as the presence of a mosque, of people in public prayer, and of typical Moslem dress, for instance—and between this evidence and certain hypotheses. In this demonstration lesson such relationships, or lack of them, seem to be noted quickly, almost instantaneously. They lead directly to the concluding activities of the lesson.

As noted above, any intellectual investigation may result in the validation or modification of the hypotheses under study as well as the invalidation of such hypotheses. Such is the case in this particular learning experience. The hypothesis that the Hausa are Moslem appears to be fairly accurate, at least on the basis of the information examined here. That the Hausa are nomads, however, seems quite questionable. Therefore we may be lead to the development of a new hypothesis. In any such investigation we may suddenly gain new insights into the subject of study as we probe deeper into the assembled evidence. These insights, posed as hypotheses, serve as occasions for further investigation.

Stating a conclusion represents an effort at closure. Determining which hypothesis is valid and which is not, which hypothesis must be modified and how, is part of this operation. But so, too, is articulating a rather precise statement that ties together the significant results of our investigation. Until a learner can state or demonstrate specifically what he has learned, we cannot assume that he has learned it. Hence, inquiry teaching should include activities which require the students to synthesize what they have learned and to state or demonstrate that synthesis.

Of course, if this were an actual classroom experience, considerably more study would be necessary before drawing any firm conclusions about the Hausa. Thus this learning activity is but a prelude to a rather extensive study that might well last two or more weeks. And the conclusions reached then will probably apply to most Hausa, not to all. While knowledge of the Hausa may not be especially relevant to many American students, the concepts, generalizations, skills, and attitudes developed or refined in working with information about them will be most useful when applied to studies of other peoples at other times in other areas of the world or even to their own cultures and ways of life.

Implications for
Inquiry Teaching

There are a number of points that should be made about the learning experience described here that go beyond the bounds of this particular lesson.

The first and most significant point is that this lesson or any inquiry-teaching lesson can proceed in a direction quite different from that planned by the teacher. Implicit in the lesson above are several objectives—to gain certain knowledge about the Hausa and, more importantly, to learn how to make inferences from data and how to use a hypothesis as a search tool in problem solving. For the most part the lesson develops in line with these objectives. Nevertheless, there is the distinct possibility that this particular lesson could at any time stray in any number of directions that are contrary to accomplishing these objectives.

One such direction might involve the analysis and evaluation of the sources and the information presented in the lesson—the dictionary list and the photographs. Imagine what track this lesson might take if some students raised questions such as "How do we know these words are really Hausa words?" or "How do we know these English translations are accurate?" or "On what basis were these words selected?" or "Who selected these words, and why these—why not others?" Similar questions could arise about the photographs. So too could questions such as "When were these taken?" or "Why this selection of photos—how typical are these scenes?" or "What was the purpose of the photographer who took these pictures?" And so on. Many questions about the data used in this lesson may be legitimately raised. What happens to the lesson if they are?

The teacher obviously has a difficult choice to make. The questions can be ignored or put aside till later—the ultimate result of which may be devastating to the questioner. Such action may be roughly equivalent to telling him, "Your views are not important so don't try to sidetrack me." or "Just follow me and I'll lead you to what you are supposed to discover!" or "You don't count!" On the other hand, the teacher may interrupt his plans in order to pursue the line of investigation suggested by these questions and then return later to the lesson as planned. Or, he may scrap his original plans altogether and allow the class to pursue the lines of investigation their questions suggest.

For a creative teacher, one skilled at inquiry teaching, a decision to "go where the kids want to go" may be perfectly natural. And the resulting learning experience can be just as productive as the one originally planned. That is, an investigation into the author or compiler or producer of any data being used, his qualifications and his purposes, his biases and methods, can help students develop some of the same thinking skills as can a study of the Hausa. Such a study may also help them better understand things like cultural bias, stereotyping, and certain principles of data collection. Learning about the Hausa might still be a possible, though somewhat incidental, part of this lesson.

Suppose questions about the data arise as soon as the teacher presents it. If the teacher wishes to let the lesson move in the direction indicated by these questions, he can have the class hypothesize about them—try to resolve them instead of hypothesize about the Hausa (a problem initiated by the teacher). That is, if the students hypothesize that the words in the dictionary list are not Hausa words or that the list was deliberately "loaded" and the words not at all typical, then they can determine ways to test the validity of these hypotheses. They may, for instance, try to find several different Hausa-English dictionaries to check the words and meanings against each other; they may consult a professor of African languages or a linguist or a Hausa himself, if possible; they may search the library for books which would reveal whether or not these words are typical. They may even collect data about the compiler of the list to determine the accuracy of and motives behind his effort. Or the students may try another approach. Any decision about the authenticity of the words or the motives of the compiler may be delayed until all the data about the Hausa can be located and examined. Then the students can determine the degree to which the words are accurate, representative, and authentic.

This same general approach might also be used in dealing with questions about the photographs. The entire learning experience will be quite a bit longer than the original lesson, especially if the teacher eventually returns to the lesson, but the students will learn valuable questioning and research skills in addition to the objectives originally planned. Should this lesson go off on a tangent, it could be a most valuable learning experience regarding data evaluation, the inquiry process in general, and the Hausa.

The original lesson on the Hausa can easily take another tangent. Suppose a student or students in the hypothesizing phase of this lesson volunteer that the Hausa are a primitive people, that they have a primitive government or economic and social system. Such a hypothesis presents an excellent opportunity to deal with a much-abused concept and a very culture-bound view of other societies and people. Instead of proceeding with the lesson as planned, a teacher interested in having students develop a more precise and less ethnocentric image of primitiveness can steer the lesson into an analysis of this concept. The students can describe what the word primitive means to them, prepare a tentative description of the concept that accounts for all the different aspects mentioned, and then apply this conceptualization first to a study of the Hausa and then to a study of other peoples and perhaps eventually to a study of their own way of life.

A study of the Hausa in this sense involves using information about the Hausa as a vehicle by which to develop a viable concept of primitiveness. The students may launch this study first by identifying all those things that are associated with "primitiveness." They can apply the resulting description to a study of the Hausa simply by asking, "Let's see if the Hausa really fit our concept of primitive!"—by trying to determine what they want to find in Hausaland that will convince them that the Hausa really are primitive. If the Hausa are primitive, then perhaps the students may expect to find hand labor rather than machinery such as tractors or cars or lathes; if the Hausa are primitive, then perhaps they wear very little clothing; if the Hausa are primitive, then maybe they live in grass huts; if the Hausa are primitive, then perhaps they engage in frequent and savage wars. And so on. The search for evidence to test these hypotheses will not only clarify and build a more perceptive concept of primitive but will also uncover a considerable amount of information about the Hausa and offer practice in using the skills of inquiry.

This same lesson can easily be "sidetracked" into different but equally or perhaps even more valuable channels. So can any lesson designed to achieve certain specific objectives. The decision as to whether or not to permit this sidetracking depends largely on the teacher. A teacher who is fact oriented or unsure of how to use inquiry teaching will probably resist such a move, and learning will proceed (he assumes) as he wishes it to proceed. A teacher who views the outcome of learning not in terms of facts but in terms of concepts, generalizations, and skills and who believes that the best learning grows out of student interest may well permit the lesson to go where the students take it. The skills he wishes to teach can be taught just as easily using content suggested by the students; but if not, other skills can be taught and the originally planned skills introduced in a later lesson. Concepts and information objectives might also be woven into the new lesson or taught at a later date. A flexible teacher, one whose security lies in knowing how to use an inquiry-teaching strategy rather than in "knowing all the answers," will find this latter course of action rewarding as well as productive and fun.

A second important point about this lesson on the Hausa and about all learning experiences built on inquiry-teaching strategies deals with the affective and cognitive aspects of inquiry—those attitude and knowledge dimensions of inquiry outlined in Chapter 1. The attitudes and values associated with inquiry are integral to this and to all inquiry-teaching lessons not just as learning tools but also as learning objectives. This particular investigation of the Hausa builds on and encourages many of the attitudes essential for effective inquiry, including the curiosity of the learner, a respect for evidence as the test for accuracy, a certain tolerance for ambiguity, a willingness to suspend final judgment, objectivity as reflected in a deliberate search for both positive and negative evidence, and a respect for the use of the rational processes. Successful inquiry teaching requires that students strive to internalize these attitudes and behave accordingly in the classroom.

The same may be said for the knowledge related to inquiring. Students must not only learn the kinds of things they need to know about knowledge, about the tools of inquiry, and about the process of inquiring, but they must also use this knowledge as they engage in inquiry-teaching experiences. Involvement in a lesson such as this on the Hausa, for example, will help the students understand the tentative, interpretive, changing nature of knowledge, for their understandings of the Hausa may be challenged by others and may change as the lesson progresses. Students should also learn to avoid sweeping generalizations based on just a skimpy list of words and a few selected photographs, for the conclusions based on this information can pertain only to some Hausa but not to all. Analytical concepts, such as *role,* may be used in this lesson and/or developed as a learning objective. So, too, can knowledge of sources of information and of how to engage in intellectual inquiry.

Inquiry relies upon command of several different types of learning tools. Inquiry teaching requires helping students not only to use these tools but also to develop and refine them and to know how to use them. While certain intellectual skills are one important set of inquiry tools, concepts are another, for concepts constitute our individual frames of reference which guide our perceptions of new data or experience and shape the kinds of meaning we are able to make of it. And so it is to concepts, the wellsprings of meaning and inquiry, that we turn next.

Concepts and Inquiry Teaching

6

What we inquire into and the meaning we give it are shaped largely by the concepts we possess. Hence concepts ought to play a very important role in inquiry teaching both as objectives of that teaching and as tools used in the course of the resultant learning. In order for inquiry teaching to be used to its fullest potential, we must understand the essential nature of concepts, be familiar with their roles in inquiring, and know how conceptualization and inquiring are related.

A concept is a mental image of something. The "something" may be anything—a concrete object, a type of behavior, an abstract idea. The image has two basic dimensions: the individual components of the concept as well as the relationships of these components to each other and to the whole.

A concept may be described by a word or phrase which conjures up the appropriate image. *War* is a word which suggests a particular mental image about a type of violence or conflict. *Dog* suggests a mental image about an entirely different concept. *Indian* and *culture* and *decision making* and *spatial interaction* suggest still other concepts. The list is almost unending.

Concepts are not mere words, however; words are only labels used to suggest concepts. Because they are so imprecise and usually mean different things to different people, words cannot thoroughly describe a specific concept. Neither can simple definitions. Concepts are much too complex for that.

A concept of *decision making,* for instance, is a complicated interrelationship of many elements. A mental image of decision making might be diagrammed as in Figure 15.[12]

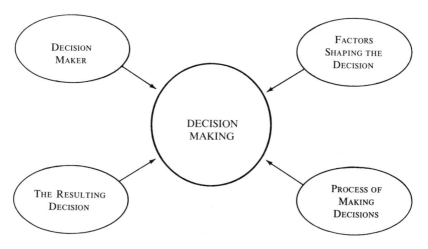

FIGURE 15

What this image suggests is that when a political scientist thinks about decision making, he thinks about who makes the decision, what factors are considered in making the decision, how the decision is made, and the resulting decision itself. The combination of these four elements forms a concept of decision making.

Yet each of these elements is itself a composite of a number of other elements. When, for example, a political scientist thinks of a decision maker, he is concerned about its individual traits (it may be a person, a group, or an institution) and its background, training, value system, and ideology. His conception may be represented by Figure 16. Or when he considers the factors shaping decisions, he may think about the information used, the influence of outside events, the expectations of the decision

---

[12] Based on a set of analytical questions reported in Edwin Fenton et al., *A High School Social Studies Curriculum for Able Students: Final Report of USOE Project—HS 041* (Pittsburgh: Social Studies Curriculum Center, Carnegie-Mellon University, 1969), p. 28.

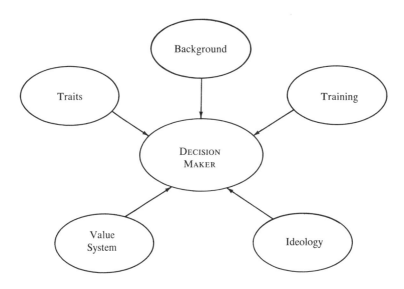

FIGURE 16

maker's clientele or constituents, the ideology of those involved as well as their frames of reference, and the goals of the institution represented. Furthermore, when he thinks about each of these items, he probably considers other even more specific aspects of them. For example, he would most certainly include in the category of information used such things as sources of this information, types of information (such as the evidence on hand, personal opinion or advice, and precedent), and the various alternatives available. In this same way, all of the major elements which constitute this concept of decision making are comprised of a number of interrelated factors. A concept of decision making in total is represented in Figure 17.

This diagram represents a mental image of a concept, but is not the only way this concept may be imagined. Different people may conceptualize it differently because of the way they go about it, the questions they ask, the nature of the data used, and the degree of intellectual inquiry they employ. Some may not include all the elements shown here, while others may include additional or different elements. A mental image is indeed an individual impression.

This concept of decision making has a multitude of functions. It may be used to study the operations of Congress or any other political decision-making body. It may be used to examine the operation of the government of the Soviet Union or of ancient Athens or Nyere's Tanzania. It may be used to analyze decision making as carried on in a

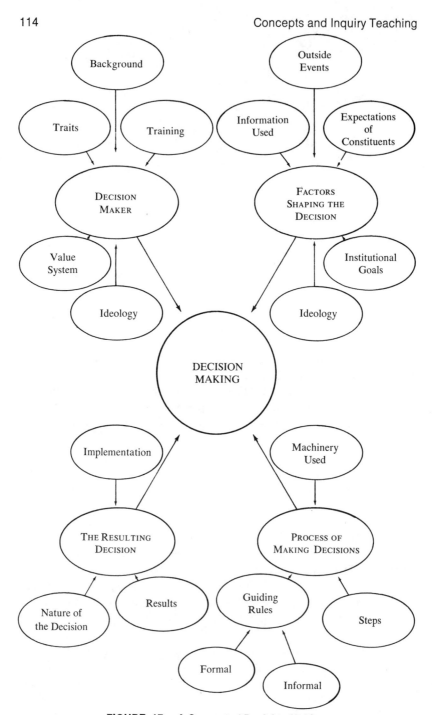

FIGURE 17. A Concept of Decision Making

specific classroom or student club, in a business or other kind of economic enterprise, or in a church or social organization. It may even be used by a student to analyze his own decision making.

The Role of Concepts in Learning

Concepts help organize data into patterns which may provide meaningful insights into that data. That is, they provide a set of interrelated categories into which evidence gleaned from data or from experience may be placed.

Concepts also generate questions which can be asked of data in order to locate evidence for these categories. Knowing a specific concept enables us to use its elements as questions with which to probe data. When found, this evidence may then be categorized in the proper "compartment" of the concept so that meaningful relationships may be identified. For example, the concept of decision making described above is composed of many interrelated categories or elements—decision maker, factors shaping the decision, guiding rules, and so on. Each of these implies certain questions that may be asked of data, such as:

> Who is the decision maker?
>
> What is he (she, it) like? . . . his traits? . . . his values? . . . his training?
>
> What procedures are used in making the decision? What machinery? What rules—formal and informal—guide this process?
>
> How is the decision implemented?

A political scientist using this concept to make sense out of data about the Cuban missile crisis might ask similar questions in order to organize the evidence into appropriate categories. Such organization enables him to identify significant relationships within this evidence and thus to make it meaningful at least in terms of decision making.

Because concepts are most useful in learning, they should be objectives of learning and thus of teaching. Much of human learning consists of conceptualizing—that is, organizing what we experience into meaningful sets of categories or concepts. We do this continuously whether in or out of school. It is done on the basis of the kinds of experiences we encounter. An average youth in the course of his own experience may conceptualize about dogs, work, school, parents, vacations, and other things with which he most likely comes into contact in his everyday living. Concepts like these and others formed in this rather random way differ greatly from person to person, but whatever form they ultimately take, they are stored in our minds for future use.

Such a collection of concepts and other experience is often referred to as a frame of reference or background of experience. Our frame of reference may be viewed as a library whose shelves hold a variety of concepts and perhaps generalizations, skills and attitudes, and even a multitude of specific facts. When we encounter new experience, we select from this library a concept that may help us make this experience meaningful. If one concept proves useless, then we select another. If none prove useful or one very inadequate, we are unable to make sense out of our new experience. Sometimes making the experience meaningful may not be of great importance to us, for we can depend on someone else to tell us what it means, to him anyway. In other instances making new experience meaningful is important, for the results may involve our security or welfare or that of others.

There is no guarantee that our students, if left to their own devices, will encounter experiences or accumulate data that will help them build a frame of reference useful for making viable sense of their future experiences, especially in today's world of rapid change. Concepts such as dog, work, school, and vacation will at best be of only limited utility in helping students deal with the wide range of social, political, economic, and cultural experiences they are bound to encounter in future years. It is precisely for this reason that our students should be deliberately helped to develop certain useful concepts as part of their mental libraries.

But which concepts should we teach? Certainly if we wish students to learn on their own, we ought to stress certain procedural or methodological concepts such as hypothesis testing, deducing, generalizing, and the like. But we also ought to stress certain substantive concepts. Yet there are literally hundreds of such substantive concepts that might be considered legitimate learning objectives for any social studies program. Which should we select?

There have been a number of significant efforts to answer this question. One of these efforts identifies and classifies certain concepts according to the social science disciplines which seem to use them most consistently.[13] According to this approach, concepts of role, group and acculturation may be classified as primarily sociological, while concepts such as region, link, and spatial interaction are essentially geographic

---

[13] An example of a discipline-based classification scheme is *A Conceptual Framework for the Social Studies in Wisconsin Schools* (Madison: Wisconsin State Department of Public Instruction, 1964).

in nature. Another effort to identify useful concepts divides them into categories of substantive ideas, methods of dealing with ideas, and values.[14] In this scheme concepts such as power, scarcity, change, conflict, and group are classified as substantive or content concepts, regardless of their parent disciplines. Causation, analysis, and interpretation are considered methodological concepts. Value concepts include empathy, the dignity of individuals, loyalty, and similar values and attitudes.

In general, however, neither of these efforts offers a practical set of criteria for identifying some of the more basic substantive concepts that might serve as instructional objectives. A more productive approach is to classify substantive concepts according to the role they play in learning. As Edwin Fenton points out, some concepts seem more useful than others in processing data.[15] Certain concepts, for example, are so all-encompassing that they are almost useless. Such concepts Fenton describes as universal and macro-concepts. Because they are so broad or all-inclusive, they must be broken down into more basic concepts before becoming useful learning tools. Culture, society, and political system are examples of such very broad concepts. These and others like them may serve best only as storage bins—purely descriptive, catch-all categories for storing certain kinds of information—or as structures for organizing courses of study, teaching units, or research. But they do not enable one to zero in on specific data with any precision at all.

A more useful type of concept is one that generates questions which are immediately helpful in analyzing data in specific detail. This type of concept is best described as an analytical concept. Decision making is such a concept, and so, too, are concepts like comparative advantage, role, landscape, market, areal distribution, change, resolution of conflict, and leadership. They may be part of larger concepts—landscape may be part of the concept of region—but they are useful in and of themselves because the questions to which they give rise are more likely to produce insights and organize data than are questions based on broader concepts. Indeed, these analytical concepts are basic tools of learning.

One possible group of basic concepts that might be considered objectives and tools for any inquiry-oriented social studies curriculum are those listed in the table below. They have been derived in part from the work of Fenton's project at Carnegie-Mellon University. The first set (I)

---

[14] The Syracuse Social Studies Curriculum Center employed this type of classification in Roy A. Price et al., *Major Concepts for Social Studies* (Syracuse: Social Studies Curriculum Center, 1965).

[15] Fenton, *High School Social Studies Curriculum*, pp. 25–27.

includes basic concepts that seem to be the foundations on which are built the second, or more analytical, set of concepts (II).

These concepts are obviously not the only concepts of import. But they are unquestionably substantive concepts useful in analyzing data. Some of them are subsumed in other concepts as, for example, link and node are essential to spatial interaction and site, situation, scale, and boundary are useful in dealing with areal distribution. Knowledge of these "smaller" basic concepts may need to preface the development of "larger" analytical concepts as goals of learning and teaching.

Regardless of how one views concepts, different types of concepts serve different roles. Some are so narrow and restricted they are hardly more than definitions. Others are so broad and all-embracing that they

SELECTED ANALYTICAL CONCEPTS

GEOGRAPHY	ECONOMICS	POLITICAL SCIENCE	SOCIOLOGY AND ANTHROPOLOGY
		I	
Site	Price	State	Role
Situation	Cost	Law	Status
Scale	Money	Sanctions	Norm
Boundary	Producer	Legislative	Family
Resource	Consumer	Executive	Group
Landscape	Goods	Judicial	Class
Link	Services		
Node			
		II	
Areal distribution	Scarcity	Decision making	Culture change
Areal association	Market	Leadership	Acculturation
Spatial interaction	Allocation	Citizenship	Assimilation
	Production		

MULTIDISCIPLINARY	
Change	Comparative advantage
Institution	Interdependence
System	Conflict
Ideology	Multiple causation

may best be used to store information and/or structure courses of study. Still others are much more analytical in nature. Some concepts are simply more useful than others in making sense out of experience, and these concepts—analytical concepts—should be considered both as tools as well as objectives of learning.

Concepts and Conceptualizing

Making things meaningful—inquiring—not only requires that students use concepts but also helps them develop their own concepts—conceptualize. Concepts cannot be handed to anyone at least not beyond the level of simple recognition. We must develop our own concepts if they are to become useful parts of our cognitive library. Inquiry teaching is designed to help us do this. Teaching concepts by inquiry teaching really means putting students into learning experiences that will facilitate their own conceptualization of any given concept.

Conceptualizing is a lengthy process. It consists basically of two steps. It requires us first to internalize a rudimentary structure of a concept, a kind of skeletal mental image incomplete in terms of all its more subtle dimensions and interrelationships but still possessing at least some basic elements. Then we must use this concept to analyze new experience or data in order to develop new insights and meaning. In so doing, we broaden and refine the initial concept by adding dimensions that become apparent during this experience. Helping students conceptualize thus requires us to guide them in engaging in these two operations.

Introducing Concepts

Concepts may be introduced in any of several ways. The teacher might tell the students his image of a given concept—outline it and then describe it by giving an illustrative example or two. Or he might present a concept as imagined and explained by a social scientist. Either way, he is only presenting or telling the students someone else's version of the concept to be studied. Such approaches can familiarize the students with the broad outlines of a concept, but they will not understand or know this concept as a result. Internalizing a concept—making it part of one's own mental library—requires use of the concept to analyze new and different bodies of content in subsequent lessons.

Involving students in learning activities that require them to invent their own conceptual images about a particular thing is a much more useful approach to introducing students to a concept and to the process of conceptualizing. Essentially it requires that the students engage in:

1. Brainstorming
2. Grouping or classifying
3. Identifying interrelationships
4. Synthesizing

Brainstorming is exactly what it implies—listing all the various implications of a word or phrase, its synonyms, or its associated terms. The purpose is to bring into view all the possible aspects of some particular idea or object, to become aware of all the various terms or behaviors associated with a particular concept. Brainstorming may suggest "thinking of all the things that are associated with x" without any specific preparation. Or, it may follow some experience that contains certain elements generally associated with the concept.

Once these associated terms or features have been listed, they must be categorized. All those terms with similar features should be placed in a single group and the group labeled with a term describing the common element.

Then the groups must be examined to determine any relationships which might exist among them. Some will appear to be elements of major significance while others may be only related to these elements.

Once these relationships have been established, the groups may be arranged—mentally or visually as in a diagram—so as to make these relationships readily apparent. This operation is really a synthesizing of all the data. The result is a concept—a mental image of what we have been working with.

Suppose for example, we wish to develop a concept of *landscape*. First, it is necessary to brainstorm about it. What do we think of when we think of landscape? Perhaps the following terms come to mind most readily:

homes	roads	billboards
trees	swings	valleys
flowers	shrubs	rivers
hills	schools	parks
erosion	telephone poles	gravel pits
tall grass	flatlands	factories

There could, of course, be many more items. But let us work with these. Are any of these similar? Do any have something in common with any other? Perhaps these could be grouped as follows:

1	2
homes	hills
schools	valleys
roads	erosion
telephone poles	flatlands
parks	trees
swings	flowers
billboards	shrubs
gravel pits	tall grass
factories	rivers

Items in group 1 are man-made. The others are natural. Yet, closer inspection suggests that these groups might be further subdivided into:

A	B	C
homes	roads	swings
schools	billboards	parks
factories	gravel pits	
	telephone poles	

D	E	F
trees	hills	erosion
flowers	valleys	
shrubs	flatlands	
tall grass	rivers	

Categories A, B, and C, contain different classes of man-made things: group A consists of structures that house people or property, B of structures that service people, and C of recreational structures. The remaining three groups characterize the natural features of landscape: D consists of things that grow on the ground, E of surface features, and F of one way surface features evolve.

What are the relationships between these groups? Perhaps the image that emerges looks something like Figure 18. This diagram is a representation of a mental image of landscape. Of course, it is incomplete in terms of how a geographer might conceptualize it. He might, for instance, add a dimension of origins to the element of surface features and perhaps a dimension of causes (meaning the kind of soil, temperature, and rainfall contributing to the growth of the vegetation) to that of vegetation.[16]

---

[16] As did John Fraser Hart in his article "Selected Concepts in the Geographic Analysis of Rural Areas," *Social Education* 30, no. 8 (December 1966): 607–609.

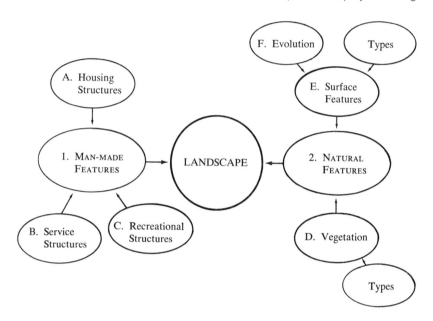

FIGURE 18.   A Concept of Landscape

Certainly the concept will be altered in time as it is used to analyze a wide variety of landscapes.

It is neither always possible nor even desirable, however, to base the introduction of a concept solely on the past experience or knowledge of the students. In many instances students lack experiences or information that enable them to brainstorm profitably about certain kinds of concepts, especially the more abstract concepts such as decision making, imperialism, or spatial interaction. Instead, students may brainstorm in response to a stimulus or learning experience designed by the teacher to provide them with examples of the concept being introduced.

Instead of having students brainstorm about the elements of landscape, for example, a teacher might present the class first with a large painting of a landscape—or a photograph or drawing of a landscape—or several paintings or pictures of different types of landscapes. The students can examine these examples and identify a number of things they see. A list of what they observe can then be made and the introduction of the concept of landscape will be well under way.

Pictures aren't the only media or resources that may be used. In introducing the concept of landscape, the teacher might provide each member of the class with a poem about a landscape, or a short essay, or even appropriate excerpts from an explorer's diary and then have the students list the kinds of things referred to as part of the landscape in each source. Or the class might look out the windows and record the different things they see as part of the landscape. A wide variety of sources are available for use in stimulating brainstorming about any particular concept. Whether a concept is introduced by the teacher's telling what he thinks it is or by students' brainstorming out of their own experiences or by class analysis of some examples of the concept, it is important to remember that this is only the first step in conceptualizing. The next step—and the crucial one—is to broaden the concept and, in the process, to internalize (learn) it.

Broadening a Concept

The second major step in conceptualizing is using the concept in whatever form it has emerged from the introductory stage to analyze new data. In terms of guiding students to develop their own concepts, this means providing them with opportunities to work with data that will not only reinforce the basic elements of the concept but will also broaden the total concept by adding new dimensions. In so doing, the basic elements of the concept may be altered considerably as experience with new data causes their modification, amalgamation, or even outright elimination. The process of refining a concept is never ending, for the more a concept is used, the more useful it becomes—and the more it is then used.

Broadening and refining concepts require the use of different kinds of data. Initially students should work with data that reflects the essential elements of the concept as they have thus far been developed. Then data having other elements commonly associated with the concept may be introduced and analyzed so that new dimensions of the concept will emerge. Finally, data that is somewhat similar but which lacks the basic ingredients of the concept may be examined, not to broaden the concept itself so much as to reinforce its essential elements by contrasting them with different data.

It is quite possible, for example, that initial efforts to conceptualize will neglect one or more dimensions of a concept which the teacher believes are important. Therefore, students must be put in touch with new data, the analysis of which will lead them to consider adding this dimension to their image of the concept. If students fail to include a category of housing structures in their initial image of landscape, for instance, and most experts believe this to be an important part of landscape, then we must provide the students with opportunities to use data in which housing structures are very prominent, such as a photograph of a housing development. As a result of this experience the students should add a new dimension to their concept in order to provide a category to account for this type of data.

Having thus guided the students to invent their own concept of landscape, we can help them broaden and refine it by having them use this concept to explain a variety of new data. The concept of landscape described above may certainly be enlarged as it is used to analyze the landscape of Brazil when studying that country in world geography, the landscape of Boston in studying an eighth-grade unit on the American Revolution, or the landscape of Europe in studying some of the work of European painters in a European history course. This same concept may even be used to make sense out of a painting by Remington, a film on Asia, a selection from *The Red Badge of Courage,* one's own front yard, the battlefield at Gettysburg, or even a photograph of astronauts on the moon. It could be used to make meaningful any particular site for any event at any time or any place in history.

Knowledge of concepts may be evaluated in a variety of ways. Whether or not a student has developed a well-defined concept of landscape, for instance, may be determined by asking him to describe it orally or in writing or even in a drawing. Or he might be asked to view three or four pictures taken in a certain area or a topographic map or an aerial photograph and then describe the landscape he sees. Should his description include comments about the major elements of landscape as developed in class, he probably has begun to internalize this concept. If he shows little recognition of these elements, however, further inquiry into the nature of landscape may be in order.

Concepts and
Inquiry Teaching

The mental operations involved in inventing a concept correspond directly to various stages of inquiring. Consequently inquiry teaching is admirably suited to helping students learn concepts and learn how to conceptualize.

There are two ways in which conceptualizing may be viewed as similar to the process of inquiring. One way is to see it as comparable to the total process itself. Brainstorming, the first step in conceptualizing, can be considered identical to the data-gathering stage of hypothesis testing. In order to resolve the implied problem "What is landscape?" we brainstormed (or collected data). We did this from memory but could have done it just as well by making a field trip and taking notes about what we saw, by reading books about landscape, or by examining photographs to identify its basic elements. Regardless of the technique, we are merely assembling evidence (or gathering data).

Categorizing involves ordering or grouping data. It is one of the major operations involved in arranging evidence for analysis. Identifying interrelationships among this evidence involves the same operations as does the final stage of hypothesis testing—analyzing data. Synthesizing a concept, putting all the elements together in a meaningful pattern, is nothing more than concluding. And applying a concept to new data—broadening the concept—is similar to the final stage of inquiry wherein a conclusion is applied to new data in order to broaden it to a generalization. In this view then, the processes of conceptualizing and inquiring are virtually identical.

A second, more precise, view of these two processes considers the initial steps of conceptualizing, referred to above as introducing a concept, as similar to what in inquiring is called hypothesizing. The final step, that of broadening the concept, is seen as similar to the stage of the inquiry process which is referred to as hypothesis testing. In this view brainstorming is nothing more than the first step in forming a hypothesis—having defined a problem, one quickly notes all the data that appears relevant. This is a sort of random listing, although it is usually quickly done and mental rather than physical in nature.

The next step in conceptualizing is categorizing. This involves the same mental operations that examining and classifying available data involve in the hypothesizing stage of inquiring. It is in essence arranging evidence for analysis. Identifying interrelationships among this evidence is really the same as the "seeking relationships and drawing logical inferences" stage of hypothesizing. Synthesizing a concept, putting all the elements together in a meaningful although quite tentative pattern, is nothing more than stating a hypothesis.

Broadening the concept, the second major step in conceptualizing, consists of the same mental operations as are involved in the hypothesis testing stage of inquiring—assembling new evidence, arranging this evidence, and analyzing it. In both instances the result is similar—a synthesis which reaffirms, modifies, or shatters the hypothesis. If the hypothesis is a tentative conceptualization, then this stage of broadening the concept (hypothesis testing) can result in making the tentative image more certain, modifying it by adding new elements and perhaps eliminating or merging other elements, or shattering it as an accurate image of reality.

Both of these views of the conceptualizing-inquiring relationship have their advantages as well as disadvantages. But the point is that the two processes are quite similar and also interrelated in that the inquiry-teaching strategy is needed to help students conceptualize. Nevertheless, even if inquiry teaching is ideally suited to the teaching of concepts, there are several important points about concepts and conceptualizing that must be understood if teaching concepts is to be productive.

Concepts do not emerge full grown. They evolve. Any effort to articulate a concept merely reveals its development at that particular moment. As it is used in subsequent learning, it will surely assume different dimensions and become increasingly complex. Concepts continually grow and change with experience.

A youngster may first describe his idea or concept of *cat* in a rather restricted way. If the family pet is an alley cat, he might describe it only in these terms. But as he grows older, he will undoubtedly come in contact with Angora cats, Siamese cats, yellow cats, tiger cats, and cats of all descriptions. His concept will broaden to take into account all the distinguishing features of these cats. Whereas he may have felt all cats are black, he begins to see them as having any number of possible colors, any length of hair, and a variety of dispositions. Yet he will still note that they meow, purr, sometimes growl, and often chase mice and birds.

What happens to this concept when the youngster one day overhears someone talking about a "cat burglar" or describing someone as a "catty" person? What happens when he goes to the zoo and sees a lion, tiger, or puma? Gradually his concept takes on new dimensions and becomes even more general in order to accomodate these examples of cat.

Concepts thus do not exist ready-made just waiting to be discovered and learned. There is no right way to imagine any given concept. They are simply inventions created individually in order to help make experience meaningful. The image of any given concept will vary according to the background or experience of whoever is conceptualizing. Even among specialists, indeed especially among them, it is impossible to get unanimous agreement about the precise nature of a given concept. Yet in many cases a number of different conceptualizations of the same idea may be remarkably similar in the basic categories included. Moreover, one person's concept of any given thing may be more valid than another's in the sense that his experience has led him to a broader, more inclusive, and thus more universally applicable concept. Descriptions of such concepts may be useful as guides to conceptualizing. However, such images should never be treated as the exact substance of what is to be learned.

Realizing that we cannot "give" anyone a concept is important. Concepts must be developed individually on the basis of one's own experiences. However, that experience can be guided. And this is precisely what teaching concepts is—facilitating student conceptualizing about a specific concept. We must bring students into contact with data or experiences that contain obvious examples of some basic, commonly accepted essentials of a particular concept and then provide them with learning experiences wherein they can broaden or refine the concept as they see fit.

Allowing students to conceptualize about anything they wish requires little if any advance planning. But facilitating student conceptualization about a specific concept requires considerable planning. In particular, the teacher must articulate his own image of the concept to be taught before he starts, or he will be unable to create learning experiences that contain clues to the concept's essential elements.

Suppose we wish to have students conceptualize about *location*. First, we must conceptualize it, perhaps in a way similar to that shown in Figure 19. In order to introduce the students to the basic elements of this concept, we might then have them engage in one or both of the following activities.

1. Each write a sentence describing the location of the teacher's desk in the room.
2. Direct a blindfolded student to a particular spot in the classroom.

All the different ways used to describe location in these activities may then be listed on the board, grouped, and synthesized into a pattern. Having already invented a basic concept of location, we can thus direct the students into examining various ways of locating objects which they ignored. Then we may have the students locate the high school in terms of each of these basic ways followed by more activities designed to give them similar practice. Periodically, of course, we will have to guide them in reflecting on the nature of their evolving concept of location so that they may gradually broaden and refine it.

To evaluate how well the students know a concept of location, we might give them an opportunity to describe verbally the location of a specific building in the town or area. If they use several of the ways included in our concept to describe location, we might assume they are beginning to internalize it. To test their ability to locate, their skill at using their knowledge or concept of location, we might have each student describe the location of his home so that a companion may locate it with a pin on a map. Only the students who find their homes accurately located may retrieve the pins.

Up to this point the concept has only been introduced. In order for it to become a useful part of the students' frames of reference, it must

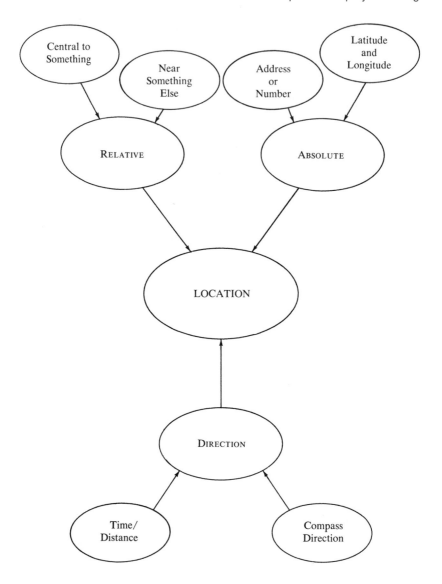

FIGURE 19.   A Concept of Location

be used in subsequent lessons. Whenever an opportunity arises for the students to locate objects or events, the activity should be structured so that they use this concept. Such reinforcement should be repeated at all succeeding grade levels regardless of the content being used.

Teaching for conceptual learning is not something in which one concept is taught one day and dropped for a new one the next. Conceptualizing takes time. It requires considerable time to introduce or formulate a concept and then repeated experience in using that concept before it can be learned (and thus taught). Teaching concepts really means planning inquiry experiences in which the same few concepts are used over and over again, always with new data and always with increasing degrees of refinement. Sometimes this teaching may focus on one particular element of the concept, following it to its most precise and refined dimensions—such as examining only the process element of decision making. Other times we might study all the major elements, first in general terms and then in increasing detail.

Of course, any concept can be taught (its learning facilitated) at any grade level although not to its fullest complexity. This does not mean that we force our own image on the students. Rather we lead them through experiences in which they articulate a concept that may only approximate our image. Their concept may not include all the dimensions we feel are important, but if the data used is appropriate, it will include some of these dimensions. Students may not use the teacher's words to describe the concept's essential elements, but they will use words meaningful to them. If given repeated contact with data in the analysis of which they can use this concept, then students will gradually broaden their image of the concept and eventually evolve a rather complex structure of interrelationships and insights. They will thus develop their own conception.

Because it is possible to teach any concept in some form does not imply that it is desirable to do so. Many concepts can be taught. Time to teach them all, however, is lacking. But so too is agreement about which are the best to teach. Hence the teacher alone must frequently decide which concept to teach. Many of us, if left to ourselves, tend to select either simple, descriptive concepts such as island, desert, or school or extremely broad concepts such as society, region, political system, and the like. Most of these concepts in themselves are of questionable value, for the chances for using them in later learning may be minimal, especially if each of us selects these concepts according to our own aims and background rather than according to any continuous pattern. On the other hand, concepts cannot be selected by someone else and then passed on to us, especially if these are merely lists of words, for the same limitations apply to us as teachers as to students: Concepts must be learned; they cannot be given.

Nevertheless, decisions about which concepts to teach must be made, and somehow all who are to teach these concepts need to be knowledgeable about those selected. Some concepts, such as location, which are both simple and basic may be introduced early and used frequently thereafter. Others such as island, grid, or house might be treated simply as definitions. But some criteria must be used to decide which of all the others to teach. One such set of criteria might be to teach those concepts that are: 1) the most teachable at a given grade level, 2) the most useful in helping students make sense out of experience, and 3) the most applicable to the particular content being used. Using criteria such as these will help eliminate from consideration concepts that are too broad or too narrow and will enable us to select those that will be most valuable to students in explaining experience.

Concepts, in sum, are keys to inquiry. They not only shape what we learn but they are shaped by what we learn. Hence, concepts must serve as objectives as well as tools of learning and teaching. Conceptualizing, making concepts, is a learner-centered process; it requires students to be active investigators instead of passive receivers. Inquiry teaching is a strategy best suited to conceptualizing in the classroom.

7

Structuring Inquiry Teaching

The key to successful inquiry teaching, or any other kind of teaching for that matter, is organization or structure, because the way we organize learning determines to a considerable extent both how and what we learn. The most productive inquiry teaching is not a hit-or-miss affair. It is well-organized teaching built directly on how one learns by rational inquiry. If we wish our students to use inquiry as well as to learn to inquire, then our teaching must be structured so that these may happen.

Inquiry teaching must encourage and facilitate, indeed require, student use of the process, skills, attitudes, and knowledge associated with inquiry. This means, in essence, structuring our teaching around a strategy of inquiry teaching. We must build learning experiences which require students to identify problems into which to inquire, to hypothesize solutions, to test their hypotheses, to draw appropriate conclusions, and then to apply these conclusions to new data over and over again as useful conceptual knowledge, skills, and attitudes evolve. Daily lessons, units, and courses of study must be organized to ensure that students will engage in these stages of inquiry.

The strategy described in the preceding pages offers a

practical framework for organizing inquiry-learning experiences, whatever their length. The essential elements of this strategy may be subsumed under the three basic components of any worthwhile learning experience—an introduction, a body, and a conclusion. The introductory phase of an inquiry lesson, unit, or course involves developing a purpose for inquiring and sometimes even hypothesizing. The body of an inquiry study is that part wherein we hypothesize, test our hypotheses, and conclude about them. The conclusion involves tying up the entire study. The introduction and conclusion are essential to an inquiry framework. No useful inquiry can be undertaken without a purpose, and the function of the introduction is to develop this purpose. Likewise, no inquiry is complete without making its meaning explicit, and this is the main function of the conclusion.

An inquiry strategy, arranged in the form of an introduction, a body of study, and a conclusion, may be used as a framework on which to organize any social studies learning experience. This strategy provides a practical guideline for structuring daily classroom lessons for all teachable students at all grade levels. It may also serve as a basic skeletal structure for units of study lasting more than one class period—anywhere from one week to several months in duration. In addition, an inquiry teaching strategy may also provide the fundamental framework for an entire course of study or sequence of courses. Use of this strategy as a way to structure lessons, units, and courses contributes greatly to the success of any inquiry teaching.

Using Inquiry to Structure Courses

Any course of study at any grade level or any sequence of courses may be organized in an inquiry fashion. Take our typical world regions or world cultures courses, for instance. These courses normally include content about several regions of the "non-Western" world[17]—including Africa south of the Sahara, southern Asia, Southeast Asia and eastern Asia. If we were to organize such a course in inquiry fashion, we might launch it by developing hypotheses about "non-Western" regions or peoples in general and then use content about each of these regions to test these hypotheses, with a series of general statements about "non-Western" cultures emerging as one final product of the inquiry.

---

[17] Many scholars and educators object to the ethnocentrism implied by the term "non-West." I agree but as yet have not been able to find a better term. Hence, "non-Western."

A course such as this might well be introduced by a short unit designed to raise questions about people as a whole and especially about the peoples of the "non-Western" world. The main question to emerge might be: What are the peoples of the "non-Western" world like? But this leads to a whole host of other basic questions such as: What do they look like? Why? How do they behave? What do they believe? And these in turn lead to questions like: Why do they do the things they do and believe what they do? How did they come to do or believe these things? What do they want to do or believe in the future? And why? Questions like these can serve as excellent problems for classroom study. Answers to them can certainly help students gain a clearer understanding of peoples from cultures different from their own and thus gain insights about people in general and themselves in particular.

Once a problem for investigation has been articulated and refined, a course may be organized in one of several ways—either in a largely cumulative fashion, or in a way best described as additive, or in some combination of the two.

An Additive Inquiry Structure

In an additive inquiry framework each major content unit is directly related to the initiatory problem and is studied independently of all other major content units. Integration of all these units occurs in a final concluding unit by, in effect, adding together the conclusions of each unit to develop a number of general statements relative to the initiatory questions or problems.

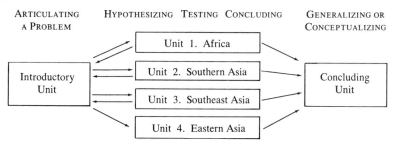

ARTICULATING HYPOTHESIZING TESTING CONCLUDING   GENERALIZING OR
A PROBLEM   CONCEPTUALIZING

FIGURE 20.   An Additive Inquiry Structure

Suppose the introductory unit is used to launch a course organized as in Figure 20. Having identified a major question to investigate— What are the peoples of the "non-Western" world like?—the students can then hypothesize an answer and proceed to test their hypotheses via in-depth study of each of the individual cultural regions to be studied. They may first focus on Africa. Here they can test their original hypothesis against content on Africa in the form of pictures, items from newspapers, or excerpts from travellers' accounts. They might commence this unit by stating, "If the peoples of the "non-Western" world are _____ [original hypothesis], then the people of Africa should be _____." Then they can study data about the habitat, ethnic groups, political structures and processes, economic features, and so on in order to test this proposition. Finally, they can bring the unit to a close by drawing conclusions about the validity of these hypotheses and by making statements about these peoples such as, "The peoples of Africa are _____ because _____. They aspire to become _____ by _____."

The students should hold these conclusions in abeyance as they turn their attention to content about a second region. Referring to the initial hypotheses, they may examine selected data about the peoples of southern Asia and hypothesize answers to these questions. Study of this region may proceed exactly like that of Africa but should end with a series of statements relative to the hypotheses about the peoples of southern Asia: "The peoples of southern Asia are _____ because _____. They aspire to become _____ by _____." Again storing these conclusions for later consideration, the students may proceed in the same manner to study content about the next region and to investigate in a similar manner each of the remaining areas to be studied.

When all the units have been studied, the students may collect their conclusions about the peoples of each region and "add them up"— integrate or synthesize them—into a series of statements generally applicable to or descriptive of all of them. Thus the students progress from the introductory unit to unit 1, then return to the ideas hypothesized in the introduction and go on to unit 2, then return to the introduction again before going on to each of the other units. Finally, they pool the conclusions developed in each unit and weave them into a concept or series of generalizations that encompass all that has been studied. This additive structure is based directly on an inquiry strategy for it includes all the basic steps of inquiring in sequence from problem to general conclusion. A course organized in this fashion has direction. It leads to a solution of a problem or to an answer to a question which is worthy of classroom investigation.

This pattern for organizing content need not be limited to a single course. A sequence of courses, indeed even an entire K–12 curriculum, may be organized in the same way. For example, let us assume that the course on world cultures just outlined is a ninth-grade course. The concepts and generalizations developed at the conclusion of this course may very well be used to initiate a study of European history in the tenth grade and of American history in the eleventh grade. A one-semester, twelfth-grade course in the humanities or on some special topics, such as world problems, ecology, or ethnic studies, might be used to test these conclusions still further. The final semester might be a synthesizing type of course in which the conclusions of each of the preceding courses are woven together and refined to develop generalizations and concepts about human behavior in all times and places with special reference to the contemporary scene.

A course or sequence of courses organized in this additive fashion offers a very high degree of flexibility, continuity, and reinforcement. It is extremely flexible because, with the exception of the introductory and concluding units, there is no special sequence in which the individual content units must be studied. Hence, units may be added, dropped, or shuffled around for any reason whatsoever (such as relevancy of content or availability of materials or student interest) without interfering with learning. Students may enter the course at almost any point without any serious handicaps. This structure also offers a certain continuity by providing a common starting point for each unit in the form of reference to the initial problem or question. It builds in periodic review and summary by using previously developed ideas, skills, and knowledge again and again. Comparison and contrast are made easy by the parallel structure of its major units and by the opportunities in the concluding unit for pooling comparable information from each of the preceding units. Above all, this framework gives the entire sequence a common purpose and a unifying thread. It allows learning to lead somewhere.

A Cumulative Inquiry Structure

A second framework on which a course or curriculum may be oganized to facilitate inquiry teaching is much more cumulative and integrative than the preceding one. A cumulative structure is one in which each unit grows directly out of and builds on the preceding unit, the entire sequence culminating in a complete synthesis of the accumulated products of all the learning experiences.

Figure 21 depicts this cumulative structure. Here the students develop a purpose for study in the introductory unit. The second unit is an in-depth study of a body of content used to hypothesize solutions to the initiatory problem and to test these hypotheses. Study of each succeeding unit offers an opportunity to modify, reject, or add to the conclusions already formed as the students progress toward conceptualizing or gen-

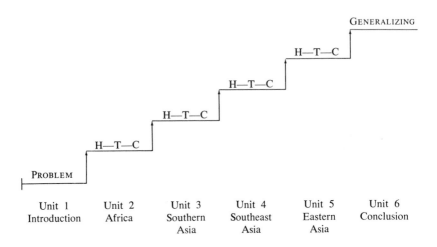

FIGURE 21.   A Cumulative Inquiry Structure

eralizing about the subject under investigation. The entire structure is built around the basic operations of inquiry teaching from problem to hypothesizing (H), testing (T), and concluding (C) to final generalizing (or conceptualizing).

The course of study about various world cultures, as described in Figure 20, might be easily organized in this cumulative fashion. The same introductory unit might be used to initiate this study. After identifying some questions for investigation, the students may engage in an in-depth study of information about culture region #1—Africa. A limited amount of data about this region and its peoples can be examined in order to hypothesize answers to the questions raised in the introductory unit. Then more data may be examined in greater detail to test the validity of these hypotheses and eventually to draw conclusions about them. These conclusions may take the form of statements to the effect that "The peoples of Africa are ———— because ————. They aspire to become ———— by ————."

The first and second units are thus organized in the same way in this framework as in the additive structure. But in the cumulative structure the students do not put aside the conclusions developed in one unit before starting the next. Instead, they treat these conclusions as hypotheses to be submitted to the test of the evidence about the peoples and cultures of the next region to be studied (southern Asia in our hypothetical course of study). As the students proceed, they perhaps modify, expand, or even drop these conclusions altogether, and they repeat this process of using the conclusions generated in one unit as hypotheses for the next. The final stage of this sequence requires the development of final conceptual or general statements embracing all the evidence examined in the preceding units.

The utility of a framework such as this is not limited to single courses. Just as is the case for the additive inquiry framework, the cumulative structure may be used to organize a sequence of several courses or even a complete K–12 curriculum. The generalizations developed at the end of one-year's course might well be treated as hypotheses to test in succeeding courses. Thus, one course may build directly on those which preceded it and lead directly to that which immediately follows.

The generalizations developed in this study of world cultures might, for example, be used as hypotheses to test in subsequent courses in European history or American history. They could be tested and appropriately modified by studying the Greeks and Romans or the inhabitants of various medieval European kingdoms. Then in the following course the conclusions that emerge in this process may be further tested by applying them to the study of colonial New Englanders, the Jamestown settlers, Southern planters, or yeoman farmers and frontiersmen. Thus the entire sequence may lead to the articulation of useful concepts and generalizations about human behavior and human beings regardless of time or place.

Because this inquiry structure is highly cumulative, it is somewhat more sophisticated, though no less flexible, than the additive inquiry framework. The major content units (such as the units on southern Asia, eastern Asia, Africa, and others cited in the above example) may be arranged in whatever order the students or teacher wish, and the students may enter the sequence at virtually any point without being seriously handicapped. Yet this framework makes advanced planning quite difficult. The teacher cannot be positive of what content to have available for the next unit until the exact nature of the hypotheses to be tested in it are known; and these are only known at the conclusion of the unit then under study. Thus, either a considerable range of data must be kept available, or the teacher must be able to predict with some accuracy what data will be needed.

This strategy is, of course, highly integrative and offers considerable opportunity for constant comparison and reinforcement. As the ideas developed in one unit are tested against new data in the next, similarities in data can be readily identified and common underlying themes or features gradually become more apparent. The entire process leads to a gradual building or broadening of knowledge and skills culminating directly in high-level intellectualization of the topic under study.

A Sequential Inquiry Structure

Although the additive and cumulative frameworks are two basic ways to organize inquiry-oriented courses or curricula, many variations can be made of them. Each of these two frameworks can be easily adapted to any type of teaching scheme whether it be large-group–small-group instruction, team teaching, or independent study. The essential elements of these two patterns may even be combined in a number of different ways. One of these variations merits particular attention. It combines the idea of cumulative modification of conclusions with the pooling of conclusions developed in the study of a number of discrete bodies of content. For our purposes here, this structure may be best identified as a sequential inquiry structure.

This sequential framework (Figure 22) requires first that a class define a problem for inquiry and examine a body of relevant data in order to hypothesize and test solutions, developing some tentative answers (conclusions) in the process. Then small groups of students or even individual students simultaneously investigate different bodies of new but related evidence in order to further test the conclusions developed by the class as a whole. Finally, all reconvene as a class to examine the conclusions of each independent inquiry and to generalize or conceptualize about the results.

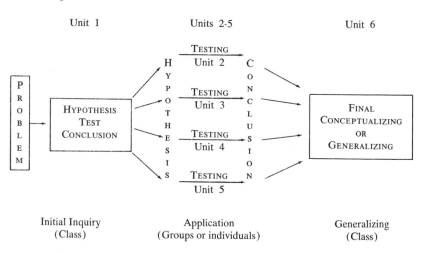

FIGURE 22. A Sequential Inquiry Structure

The sequential inquiry structure may be used to organize a study of virtually any topic or theme. The study of "non-Western" cultures described above may easily be organized along these lines. The students can develop a problem and then study as a class one cultural region in order to hypothesize solutions and test them. Their conclusions could then be tested further by small groups, each studying a different region of the "non-Western" world. The concluding unit brings them back together to share the results of their investigations and to develop some general statements applicable to all the regions examined.

This same structure might also be used to study the causes of wars in which the United States has been involved. Students could hypothesize by discussing reasons for American involvement in Indochina. Then, to see if these reasons hold for all U. S. wars, the class might study how another American war—the War of 1812, for instance—came about. After the list of reasons is appropriately revised, each student or group of students may examine a different American war in order to see if the hypothesized list is valid for all wars. Reconvening as a class, the students may share the results of each inquiry and may develop a comprehensive list of causes. Such a list may be used later to analyze the causes of other wars in world history and perhaps even conflicts of a less violent nature.

A more sophisticated variation of this structure might be employed to organize a study of revolutions. Such a study might commence with a brief look at some contemporary event that purports to be revolutionary such as a campus disturbance, a student strike, an invention, a discovery, or a significant achievement such as the moon landing. Students could hypothesize about the nature of revolutions—What are they like? What causes them? What kind of results do they have?—and build a simple conceptual model. Then the class might examine evidence about the American Revolution in order to test, broaden, and revise the hypothetical model.

At this point the class could be divided into several teams, each examining data about a different revolution in order to test the hypothesized model. They could choose from data about the French Revolution, the Glorious Revolution, the Russian Revolution, the Chinese Revolution of 1911, or the independence revolutions in Latin America. The results of these could then be pooled and the hypothetical model revised. Each student could then be assigned to investigate on his own yet another revolutionary event such as the European Renaissance, the Reformation, the Harlem Renaissance, the agricultural, scientific, industrial, and atomic revolutions, the civil rights revolution, revolutions in architecture, music, and transportation, and so on. The results of these independent investigations could again be pooled and a comprehensive model developed. Finally, the students could study several existing theories of revolution—such as that presented by Crane Brinton in *Anatomy of a Revolution*—in order to evaluate their own model and refine their own concept of revolution.

Each of these three structures is built on the inquiry-teaching strategy outlined in the preceding chapters. All are directly related to how people learn on their own. The additive structure reflects the way in which people pool the results of discrete but essentially similar experiences that occur over a long period of time (usually interrupted by numerous totally unrelated learning experiences). The cumulative structure approximates the more deliberate, step-by-step process by which individuals tackle problems of direct concern to them. The sequential framework, which is often used by those engaged in theorizing about selected questions or problems, represents a practical combination of the essential elements of both of these approaches.

A teacher might wish to use all three of these frameworks in the same course. If so, the additive framework may be used to structure the first course or segment of a course so that students can gain experience in using the skills of inquiry without getting too deeply involved in the complex interrelationships of the content. The cumulative framework may then be used so that the students can experience the progressive aspects of working out solutions to problems involving closely interrelated data. Finally, the sequential framework may be used to provide an opportunity for completely independent inquiry—the necessary culminating experience in any course or curriculum designed to teach students how to learn on their own.

Using Inquiry Structures to Organize Units

A basic difference between a unit of study and a course is the length of time devoted to each. A course is usually one semester or one year in length. A unit lasts anywhere from one week to several months. Most courses, in fact, consist of a number of units. In terms of structure, a unit is nothing more than a mini-course. To be effective, it must be organized just like a course—that is, it must have an introduction and a conclusion as well as a body of content. The same inquiry frameworks for structuring courses can and should be used to organize units for inquiry teaching. Repeating the specific characteristics of these three frameworks is unnecessary, but a description of several different sample units built on one or more of them may be helpful.

Let us take a unit on a "non-Western" culture, for example. Suppose we wish to organize a five-week study of Africa, which is one of a series of units on various "non-Western" cultures. Suppose further that the focus of the unit is to be people and that the purposes of the study are not only to learn something about people and their culture but also to practice skills of intellectual inquiry and to develop general statements about Africa that may be treated as hypotheses for testing in the next unit which is to be on southern Asia.

Our unit might be introduced by helping students articulate their image of Africans—in response, perhaps, to a series of pictures that challenges them to pick out only those people who are inhabitants of this region or perhaps in response to the question: "What comes to mind when you think of an African?" The stereotyped view that is certain to emerge may then be challenged by some statistics or a film that depicts the wide variety of peoples who call this region home. The students will express curiosity about these people and perhaps even about this material. From here they can move immediately to a study of some specific African peoples and cultures.

Our hypothesized "typical African" may be tested against informa- tion about several different groups of Africans, each selected for study because its culture represents a feature common to many Africans. The students may first study the Hausa of Nigeria, hypothesizing about the nature of these people on the basis of limited evidence and then testing these hypotheses by analyzing Hausa music, art, folklore, tradition, social customs, and so on. Then they may draw some conclusions about the Hausa relative to these hypotheses—either they are valid, or they need to be added to, modified, or dismissed.

Thereupon, the students may turn their attention to another group, perhaps the Ganda of Uganda. Again, they may hypothesize about these people and then test their hypotheses by analyzing the behavioral and physical expressions of Ganda culture. Conclusions may then be drawn about their validity. Similar studies can be made of other Africans, too, such as the Luba and the Kikuyu.

Finally, our unit may draw to a close by having the students pool their conclusions regarding each group of people and relate them to their original image of typical Africans. Certainly this image will need to be modified in view of the evidence just examined. Important generaliza- tions about Africans will result. Although these represent the conclusion of this unit, they may also be treated as hypotheses about peoples of the "non-Western" world in general and submitted to the test of data about the inhabitants of Southeast Asia in a following unit.

Such a unit is built on an additive framework. It proceeds from an introduction that generates a problem for investigation to hypotheses that are tested by a number of different sets of data—in this case data about different groups of Africans. Then the conclusions of each test are pooled and generalizations derived. In diagram form this unit might be depicted as in Figure 23.

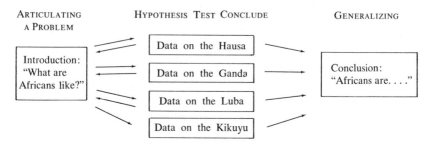

FIGURE 23.   A Unit Built on an Additive Inquiry Structure

By way of another example, suppose we wish to organize an inquiry-oriented unit about leadership in America along the lines of a sequential framework. Such a unit might be introduced by having students articulate a problem for study—Why do some people become leaders and others not? The entire class might attempt to identify why they think certain of their schoolmates have attained positions of leadership in school affairs—the head cheerleader, the president of the dramatics club or student council, the football captain, the features editor of the school paper, and so on. Evidence could be sought by checking records and perhaps by interviewing these leaders and other students. The class could conclude this phase of the inquiry by making some general statements as to how people become leaders. In turn, these statements may be considered hypotheses for further study.

Thereupon each student could be assigned to look into the life of one recognized American leader. Representatives of all aspects of life might be studied—from the field of politics: George Washington, Carl Stokes, Thaddeus Stevens, William Jennings Bryan, John F. Kennedy; from the arts: Frank Lloyd Wright, George Gershwin, Earl (Fatha) Hines; from business: Andrew Carnegie, Henry Ford; from other areas of society: the Wright brothers, Martin Luther King, Susan B. Anthony, Jonas Salk, Neil Armstrong, Daniel Hale Williams, and even Wyatt Earp. Each student could attempt to test the class statements about what qualities determine leadership by seeing to what extent these factors are evident in the career of his or her subject.

Upon reconvening and pooling all conclusions, the class might develop a general list of leadership factors which can be checked against the original hypothesis or against excerpts from Machiavelli's essay on leadership, *The Prince*. Or students might be asked to apply their conclusions by preparing a critique of James MacGregor Burns' description of Franklin D. Roosevelt as both "a lion and a fox." Or they might even use the criteria they develop to appraise the potential or career of a prominent local or national figure.

This unit could vary in length depending on the amount of time allotted to the independent research phase and on the number of students who must report on their findings. Regardless of its length, however, the unit may be considered an example of the sequential inquiry structure. The students develop a problem, work out and test a tentative solution to the problem, and then investigate one or more new bodies of data relative to this same problem before pooling their conclusions and revisions and applying some general statements regarding the initial problem. Diagrammatically, the unit might look like that in Figure 24.

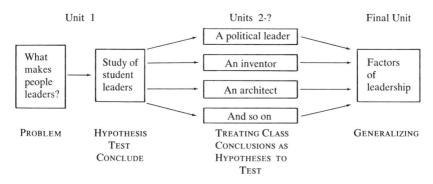

FIGURE 24. A Unit Built on a Sequential Inquiry Structure

Either of the units discussed above can be organized just as easily along the lines of any other inquiry framework. The point is that a good unit of study must be as carefully structured as a good course of study. And inquiry units may be organized just like inquiry-structured courses. The only difference between units and courses is the scope of what is being studied and the time devoted to this study. An inquiry-structured course should consist of a number of similarly structured units.

Using Inquiry to Structure Daily Lessons

The real nub of inquiry teaching is what goes on daily in the classroom. Like a good unit or course, daily inquiry teaching doesn't just happen. It, too, is structured. Its framework may be written down or memorized but, nevertheless, there is one. Carefully designed daily learning experiences built on a strategy like that described in the preceding chapters are the real essence of effective inquiry teaching. Teachers, especially those inexperienced in inquiry teaching, cannot use this strategy and expect that students will respond without some guidance.

This guidance is not provided in the form of the traditional course or unit curriculum guide—the three-columned listing of content, activities, and suggested materials. Such guides are really of little use in the classroom. They fail to tell us how and when we should do what must be done, knowledge of which is essential to everyday teaching. At best, such guides are only the beginning of curriculum development, not the final product. At worst they serve to lull school administrators into thinking that they know what is going on in "their" classrooms. That the vast majority of guides like these are filed in some remote spot to gather dust almost as fast as they are produced is not surprising.

The kinds of guides required in inquiry teaching are those which specifically delimit what is to happen throughout the entire process. This means plans for each learning experience of which the unit is comprised. Daily lesson plans. These plans represent the most immediate and useful level of structured inquiry teaching. Just as every curriculum consists of courses and every course of units, so too must every unit consist of specific plans for each daily learning experience included in it. Such plans should describe the major operations to be performed by teacher and students alike in order to progress from one stage of learning to the next.

These daily guides or lesson plans are more than scratch outlines. They do not consist of notes such as "discuss," "show film," "cover," and so on. Nor do they merely list activities in which students may engage. Instead, because they are built on an inquiry-teaching strategy, they describe not only the key operations to be performed by the teacher and students in order to move from one intellectual level to the next but also the key statements or actions of the students which will reveal when such moves may be made. Preparation and implementation of plans that achieve these objectives within the framework of inquiry-structured units and courses will make inquiry teaching a reality.

The specific type of format for these daily plans may vary according to what seems to work best for a particular teacher. They may be as specific and detailed as is necessary to facilitate the desired learning experiences. For teachers unaccustomed to inquiry teaching, the plans should be quite detailed—written as if to direct another teacher how to conduct the lesson. But if the teacher has a feel for inquiry teaching and knows how to use the process to its fullest potential, his plans need not be nearly so elaborate.

Planning specific daily lessons begins not so much with the content as with a structure of the process of how that content is to be used (a model of inquiry teaching). Let us assume we are to teach the unit on Africa that is part of a course on "non-Western" cultures. Let us assume further that this is the first unit in the course and that we want, therefore, to focus on the peoples of Africa—who they are, what they are like and why, and what they are becoming—in order to develop some conclusions to treat later as hypotheses for studying peoples of Southeast Asia and other culture areas. We want to study four different African peoples in depth, devoting about five days to each. After designing an introductory unit in which the students articulate a problem for investigation—What are Africans like?—and hypothesize about it, we may then proceed to study the first of the peoples we have selected, the Hausa of northern Nigeria. This five-day study might be organized as follows:

1. PROBLEM:	We think Africans are. . . .	
	What are the Hausa like?	First Day
2. HYPOTHESES:	The Hausa are. . . .	
3. TESTING THE HYPOTHESES:	If the Hausa are. . . , then I expect to find . . . (specific examples or evidence of these features).	Three Days
4. CONCLUSION:	The Hausa are. . . .	Final Day

This study may have many objectives. Suppose, though, that as a result of this inquiry we want the students to know something about these people, what they are like and why, to practice certain skills of intellectual inquiry, and to be willing and indeed anxious to work together and inquire. Some of the knowledge developed may even help the student better understand his own way of life and himself, why and how his life is arranged as it is. We can probably complete the first two steps of the inquiry on the first day of class and then devote three days to testing the hypotheses and a final day to drawing conclusions. The lesson plans[18] for each of the five days might be as follows:

---

[18] The first column describes what the teacher should do. The second column indicates what the students may say or do in response. Not all possible student responses are indicated here. It should not be assumed that the responses indicated here are accurate; they represent only what students usually (or probably) will say.

These lessons are based on materials developed by Project Africa, a social studies curriculum center at Carnegie-Mellon University under a contract with the United States Department of Health, Education and Welfare, Office of Education. Copies of the original Project materials may be obtained from the ERIC Document Reproduction Service, The National Cash Register Company, 4936 Fairmont Avenue, Bethesda, Maryland 20014.

FIRST DAY

DEFINING A PROBLEM AND HYPOTHESIZING

Objectives:

Given a list of words common to the Hausa, to infer and state in writing at least three possible characteristics of their way of life.

When paired with another student, to be willing to engage in co-operative investigation of given data.

Materials:

list of selected Hausa-English words

TEACHER	STUDENTS

Defining a Problem

1. Refer to the student decision (in the preceding lesson) to study some specific African peoples in order to answer the questions: What are Africans like? Why? What are they becoming? Have students refer to their original hypothesis about Africans in general.

2. Have the students refer to the map of Selected Ethnic Groups in Africa and to locate the Hausa. Write *Hausa* on the board. What are the Hausa like?

Africans are. . . .

Hypothesizing

3. Point out that one way to find out about any group is to study their language. People use words to describe things with which they are familiar (or of which they are aware). For

TEACHER	STUDENTS
example, we use the word *automobile* to describe a type of vehicle. Any people which has the word *automobile* in its language probably has or knows about this type of vehicle.	
4. Write on the board:	
net sinker line bait oar hook	
Ask: What can we tell about a people who use these words frequently?	These people probably are associated with fishing. They must live near some bodies of water—lakes, rivers, oceans.
If we had some Hausa words, we could do the same thing to figure out what they are like.	
5. Pair the students. Distribute one copy of the list of Hausa words to each pair. Direct them to look at the Hausa words (and the English meanings) and list three characteristics of the Hausa or of their way of life.	The following characteristics may be suggested: religious—Moslem traders farmers superstitious have a well-organized government
6. Have the students report what they listed. Write these on the board. As each characteristic is written, require the students to cite evidence from the word list that suggests this characteristic.	

Stating the Hypothesis

7. Have the students write a statement describing what they think the Hausa are like.	The Hausa are. . . .

TEACHER	STUDENTS

Testing the Hypotheses

Identifying Needed Evidence

8. Have the students identify the kinds of evidence they need to find if their guesses about the Hausa really are accurate. Ask: If the Hausa are Moslem, then what kind of evidence do you want to find to convince you they really are Moslem? Repeat this question for other characteristics.	If the Hausa are Moslem, then we want to find evidence of: mosques the *Koran* in use veiled women people bowing down praying

SECOND DAY

TESTING THE HYPOTHESES

Objectives:

Given a filmstrip of the Hausa, to identify information (evidence) relevant to the hypotheses being tested.

Given this filmstrip, to make additional inferences (hypotheses) about the Hausa and their way of life.

To derive satisfaction in finding evidence to support hypotheses about the Hausa as evidenced by a willingness to participate in class discussion.

Materials:

filmstrip: *The Hausa of Northern Nigeria*

TEACHER	STUDENTS

Review

1. Have the students refer to the hypotheses to be tested and some of the evidence needed to prove their accuracy.	The Hausa are. . . . We need to find. . . .

TEACHER	STUDENTS
2. Have the students list some possible sources where such evidence might be found or secured.	From: books speakers (a Hausa perhaps) films

Collecting Evidence

3. Introduce the filmstrip. Direct the students to select a hypothesis to test, to decide what evidence they want to see, to verify it, and then to look for this evidence in the filmstrip.	The filmstrip shows photos of the landscape, housing, economic activities, and so on.
4. Project the filmstrip slowly. Encourage students to comment on what they see. Stop the filmstrip to discuss their observations; reverse the filmstrip when necessary.	

Arranging and Analyzing Evidence

5. At the conclusion of the filmstrip have the students go over their hypothesized characteristics to determine, on the basis of the evidence just seen, which seem accurate, which do not, and which remain yet untested. Require evidence from the filmstrip to support student opinions.

Developing a Tentative Conclusion

6. Have the students each write a statement describing what they feel are probably the major characteristics of the Hausa and their way of life.	Based on the evidence we have seen so far the Hausa are. . . .

TEACHER	STUDENTS

Developing New Hypotheses

7. Have the students suggest any new characteristics of the Hausa suggested by the film-strip but not yet mentioned. Have them list what other characteristics still need to be tested further.

May suggest:
large urban areas
industry
"modernizing"
May suggest:
superstition

Testing Hypotheses

Identifying Needed Evidence

8. Have the students identify the evidence needed to verify each of these hypotheses.

If the Hausa are superstitious, then we want to find. . . .

THIRD DAY

TESTING THE HYPOTHESES

Objectives:

To know that a people's folk literature expresses and reveals what they value and respect as well as what they do not value or respect by identifying in some selected Hausa folk literature at least three things which the Hausa value.

Given some Hausa folktales, to identify evidence relevant to the hypotheses being tested.

Given some Hausa folktales, to make at least three inferences about the nature of the Hausa way of life.

To derive satisfaction from finding evidence to support hypotheses about the Hausa by expressing a willingness to inquire further into data about these people.

Materials:

(1) recording of a Hausa folktale
(2) copies of several Hausa folktales
(3) reading about the life of a Hausa girl

TEACHER	STUDENTS

Review

1. Have the students refer to the hypotheses still to be tested and some of the evidence needed.

large urban areas
industry
"modernizing"
superstition

Collecting Needed Evidence

2. Introduce the folktales. Point out that all peoples tell stories that illustrate how they should or should not behave or that reveal qualities to be admired or condemned. Have the students suggest some stories that do these things, and have them tell what they mean.

Students may suggest some Dr. Seuss stories, for example.

3. Note that the Hausa also have stories that do the same thing. One story is about two frogs. Tell them to listen to the story to find out what it is about. Play the recording and discuss it.

This story is about two frogs who fall into a bowl of cream and they cannot get out. One gives up and drowns. The other kicks so hard he churns the cream into butter, climbs on the ball of butter, and escapes.

Arranging and Analyzing Evidence

4. Have the students discuss which hypotheses this story supports or refutes. What does this story tell us about the Hausa?

Some type of milk-giving animal is around. A cow, perhaps? They live near water or marsh. At least its wet sometimes.

It may be necessary to replay the story a second or third time. Have the students identify the "good guy" and the "bad guy" to note the personal traits the Hausa seem to value.

Perseverance and hard work characterize the "good guy." Helping yourself counts!

TEACHER	STUDENTS

Collecting Needed Evidence

5. Divide the class into small groups. Give each group a different Hausa folktale. Have each group read their folktale to find any evidence to support or refute the hypotheses they are now testing.

Arranging and Analyzing Evidence

6. Have the groups report. Have the class decide which hypotheses are strengthened and which still seem doubtful on the basis of this evidence. Which hypotheses are still untested?

Developing New Hypotheses

Have the students report what new characteristics of the Hausa are suggested by this evidence.	The Hausa seem to value cleverness or shrewdness.

Testing Hypotheses

Identifying Needed Evidence

7. Have the students determine what evidence is needed to verify these new or as yet untested hypotheses.	If the Hausa are . . . , then. . . .

Collecting Needed Evidence

8. Distribute the reading about the life of a Hausa girl, and have the students seek out relevant evidence in this reading as independent work.

FOURTH DAY

TESTING THE HYPOTHESES

Objectives:

Given additional data about the Hausa, to identify evidence relevant to the hypotheses being tested.

Given this data, to make additional inferences about the Hausa and their way of life.

To be willing to respond in class as evidenced by volunteering to participate in class dialogue.

Materials:

(1) reading about the life of a Hausa girl
(2) list of Hausa proverbs

TEACHER	STUDENTS

Arranging and Analyzing Evidence

1. Have the students refer to some of the hypotheses being tested. Have them report what they found in the reading to support or refute any of these hypotheses or any of the characteristics mentioned earlier. Write the accepted hypotheses on the board.

Developing a Tentative Conclusion

2. Refer the students to the statements they wrote on the first day. Have them rewrite these statements to include what, on the basis of their study so far, they believe are the major characteristics of the Hausa and Hausa way of life. | Based on the evidence we have seen so far, the Hausa are. . . .

TEACHER	STUDENTS

Developing New Hypotheses

3. Note any as yet untested or doubtful hypotheses. What new characteristics of the Hausa are suggested by the reading?

Testing Hypotheses

Identifying Needed Evidence

4. Have the students determine what evidence they need to verify these hypotheses.

If the Hausa are . . . , then we need to find. . . .

Collecting Needed Evidence

5. Distribute the list of Hausa proverbs. Point out that these are like the stories—they illustrate desirable behavior and thus reflect the value system of a people. Have students suggest any similar sayings they know.

(A list of proverbs grouped by themes.)

Perhaps:
    A penny saved is a penny earned.
    An apple a day keeps the doctor away.

6. Divide the class into groups. Direct each group to analyze a different set of proverbs to (1) find the theme of the set, (2) indicate what this tells about the Hausa, and (3) tell to what extent this evidence supports or refutes the hypotheses being tested.

Arranging and Analyzing Evidence

Students work in groups to prepare lists.

TEACHER	STUDENTS

8. Have the groups report. Write the characteristics they report on the board. Have the students evaluate the statement they made earlier in the light of this new evidence. Have them evaluate the hypotheses being tested.	Some new characteristics may be:
	
	    strong family ties
	    thrift
	    fatalism

Developing a Tentative Conclusion

9. Have the students revise their statements in the light of this analysis. Then distribute the newspaper article describing Hausa life. Direct the students to study it as independent work to see how accurate it is (in terms of what they now know about the Hausa). Each student should list three or four statements they consider to be inaccurate.	Based on the evidence we have examined so far, the Hausa are. . . .

FIFTH DAY

DEVELOPING A CONCLUSION

Objectives:

To be able to describe at least five major features of the Hausa and their way of life.

Given all the data thus far used, to be able to synthesize it into a unique communication descriptive of the Hausa.

Given an article by a journalist, to be able to judge its accuracy by identifying three accurate statements and three inaccurate statements in it.

To derive satisfaction from developing an accurate description of the Hausa as evidenced from questions asked about the Hausa.

Materials:

newspaper article about the Hausa

TEACHER	STUDENTS

Applying Conclusions to New Data and Generalizing

1. Have the students report the inaccuracies they found in the newspaper article. Require evidence to support their opinions.	Regardless of which inaccuracies are cited, it is the evidence cited by the students in support of their views that is the focus of this lesson.
2. Have the students suggest what they think are the five most important characteristics of the Hausa. (They should use the statement prepared in the preceding lesson, any notes they have, and the ideas generated in analyzing the newspaper article.) List these characteristics on the board.	
3. If necessary have the students group similar characteristics together and label each group.	
4. Have the class agree on a statement that describes as accurately as possible (based on their study) what the Hausa are like.	Based on the evidence we have examined, the Hausa are. . . .

Referring to the Original Unit Hypothesis to Restate the Problem

5. Have the students refer to their original image of Africans articulated in the introduction to this unit. To what extent does this description of the Hausa fit this image?	
6. How typical of all Africans are the Hausa? What can be done to find out?	Study other groups of Africans about whom we have heard. How about the Kikuyu? the Tuareg? the Egyptians? the . . . ?

The one-week study of the Hausa suggested in these lesson plans is a very simple study, indeed. Such a study might very well move in a number of directions quite different from that suggested here. Different kinds of content and materials could be used. Any number of different objectives could be sought. However, the important thing here is the way in which this particular set of lessons is organized. These five days are structured on an inquiry-teaching strategy. The students are involved in learning experiences which require them, after defining a problem for investigation, to hypothesize an answer, to test this answer against relevant data, to draw some valid conclusions on the basis of their testing (not on the basis of what someone else says), and finally to apply these to new data and refine their own conclusions. These steps are the essence of inquiry. If executed as suggested here, this study will be an example of inquiry teaching. The conclusions that finally evolve can be used as hypotheses to test against data of another African people if the unit is organized according to the cumulative model. If the unit is organized on the additive model, these conclusions might be held in abeyance until a separate study of another people is made.

This same daily strategy may be used to teach any conceptual knowledge or intellectual skill objectives. It may also be used to get at the affective domain, specifically at value clarification. Variations may be made on this procedure too, but nevertheless, it may serve as a convenient framework for teaching students how to inquire while using inquiry strategies.

Summary

Inquiry teaching has many facets. Of these, its organization or structure is most crucial. If a course or unit of study does not require students to define a problem, hypothesize answers to it, test these hypotheses against all kinds of data, draw reasonable conclusions, and apply these to new data and synthesize some valid generalization or final conclusion, inquiry is not likely to occur in the daily classroom learning experiences. If daily lessons are not carefully designed to require students to engage in these same mental operations, inquiry surely will not occur. Carefully planned lessons using an inquiry strategy are essential to effective inquiry teaching.

Daily plans may be more or less elaborate than those outlined above. It is possible that considerable successful experience in using an inquiry strategy will obviate the necessity for such detailed plans. But the newcomer to this strategy needs much detail. Otherwise he may get so bogged down with the content that the lessons may easily revert to lecturing and memorizing. Detailed plans have another advantage, too.

Implications for Teaching

8

The key to successful inquiry teaching is what happens in the classroom. All the curriculum building, unit writing, and lesson planning in the world, even if they are based directly on an inquiry strategy, will be for naught unless students daily engage in learning experiences that require them to use the skills and processes of intellectual inquiry. Therefore most teachers and students will have to behave differently than they do now, doing different things, using materials in a different way, and seeking different objectives, if inquiry teaching is truly to become a classroom reality.

Inquiry teaching is quite different from the more traditional expository teaching that characterizes many social studies classrooms. Inquiry teaching is process rather than content oriented. It is conceptual instead of factual in emphasis. It is student centered, not teacher centered. It is active not passive. Inquiry teaching does not treat content as an end in itself but rather uses it to accomplish purposes of more far-reaching significance. It is different in more subtle ways too. Teachers who wish to use inquiry teaching to its fullest potential must be aware of these essential differences and of the implications of these for teaching, for their students, and for themselves.

Using
Inquiry Teaching

It is important to realize that inquiry teaching is only one way of teaching. It may be neither desirable nor possible to use all the time, nor may it be best suited for accomplishing all the different objectives we may wish to achieve. While inquiry teaching is obviously not the best way to cover large amounts of content in short periods of time, it may be the most useful way to facilitate the learning of large amounts of information in a relatively short time. Above all, inquiry teaching is almost certainly the best way to facilitate the development of conceptual knowledge and intellectual skills, to improve study skills, and to help clarify attitudes and values. Inquiry teaching ought to be used when these kinds of objectives have been selected for classroom instruction.

Time Requirements

Inquiry teaching is more than a one-period undertaking. More often than not it requires many class periods to complete. One period may be devoted entirely to clarifying a problem or raising questions for investigation. One or two more may be spent in refining hypotheses. Assembling, arranging, and analyzing sufficient evidence to test the validity of the hypotheses may take three, four, or a dozen or more class periods, while drawing meaningful conclusions about the entire investigation may well require several additional periods. Inquiry teaching takes considerable time.

As a result, it is most difficult to determine on the basis of one class observation or on the perusal of one daily lesson plan whether or not inquiry teaching is really in operation. Making this decision requires familiarity with the entire strategy being used or continued observation over a sequence of learning experiences. Seeing one or two techniques in operation is not enough to know what particular strategy is being employed. Rather, one must know how the various techniques are interrelated to determine whether students are engaged in inquiring or memorizing or whatever. If the same technique is observed day after day, then inquiry teaching is probably not being used. But if the lesson involves student manipulation of content, inquiry teaching is probably in operation.

Because inquiry teaching takes considerable time, it cannot be used to become familiar with wide ranges of factual information in short periods of time. Thorough investigation of a problem or question, whether it be of a substantive or value-laden nature, requires time. If the major objective is to be able to recognize names, dates, laws, lists of products, and other data, inquiry teaching will be too time-consuming. But if the purpose is to develop conceptual knowledge, to clarify values, or to refine the skills of learning to learn and simultaneously learning some facts, it will be most useful.

Inquiry teaching requires that content be carefully selected. Since this content is used in depth for a relatively long duration, detailed coverage of many large areas of content is impossible. But detailed study of a few subjects in depth is not impossible. A study of political leadership may be built around an intensive study of only four or five presidents, for example, instead of all of them. This small sampling does not mean that less content per se is being used. Far from it. A study of one president in depth may involve much more factual information than a sweeping survey of ten or more, but this inquiry approach does permit less sweeping coverage than does traditional expository teaching. Thus, using inquiry teaching means that coverage of many topics must be eliminated in favor of depth studies of a few, that a considerable amount of content which is usually covered in many courses must be replaced with new content in depth on a more limited number of topics.

Types of Instructional Techniques

The fact that inquiry teaching is selective does not mean that some techniques are exclusive to it while others are forbidden. Every instructional technique can be useful in inquiry teaching. There is, for example, a place for the lecture. Students periodically need data to test their hypotheses, against which to apply some newly developed conclusions, and perhaps even to generate questions for further investigation. This data may be communicated through a variety of media—perhaps a book or film, a record or tape, or even some type of oral presentation such as a report or lecture. For example, a lecture may be the best way to put students in touch with data they need but cannot locate on their own; a lecture may be used when we want the students to devote their time to arranging and analyzing data rather than collecting it; or a lecture might be used to help students refine their skills of separating the relevant from the irrelevant, or the skills of selective listening.

Lectures and all other instructional techniques may serve a variety of purposes. It is the purpose for which a particular technique is used that determines whether or not it should be included in inquiry teaching. A clue to the purpose of a technique is what the students do as a result of its use. What students do with the content of a lecture, for example, determines whether or not this technique is being used as part of an inquiry strategy. If the students merely commit the substance of the lecture to memory and then reiterate it on a later test, an inquiry strategy is not being employed. Or if lectures are given day after day, then it is doubtful that inquiry teaching is in operation. But if the students use the data from a lecture to build a hypothesis or to test a hypothesis, if they work with the data, then the lecture plays a very legitimate role in inquiry teaching.

There are, however, certain instructional techniques which are better suited to inquiry teaching than to other strategies. Probably the most important of these and certainly the most crucial is that of questioning because it is questions that guide students through the process of learning by inquiry. Inquiry questions reach far beyond those utilized by expository teaching both in form and degree of sophistication. Questions in inquiry teaching do not require just mere repetition or description of the facts being studied. On the contrary, they emphasize the "why" much more than the "what," the "so what," as well as the "how." Questioning is a technique for guiding learning.

In expository teaching questioning usually serves only as a check to see if the students can repeat what was contained in the text or given in the lecture or discussed in class. In inquiry teaching, however, questions such as these are but the first stage in learning, for we use additional questions of all types to help students move through the entire learning experience. Some questions are useful in developing hypotheses (What would happen if . . . ? or How do you account for . . . ?). Building on the responses to these, we can ask additional questions to identify needed evidence (If this is true, then what do we expect to find?), to collect evidence (What does the picture show?), to clarify or interpret evidence (What does it mean?), to categorize or note patterns (Which of these seem to have something in common?), and so on. Each kind of question builds on the responses and insights developed in answer to the preceding questions and then seeks to probe for new insights and meanings. Thus in inquiry teaching, questions facilitate learning by guiding one through the process of intellectual inquiry from problem to conclusion. They lead somewhere rather than simply seek a recounting of what is already believed to be true.

The ways in which these questions and questions like them may be used to guide inquiry may vary, of course. Ideally the students should be asking the questions. One way of inducing student-initiated questions is to confront the students with a problematic situation, allow them to develop a problem for investigation, and permit them to proceed unguided to seek a resolution that satisfies them. We need ask no questions at all. The entire burden of inquiring is left to the students. Such an approach is highly nondirective and can be quite useful, especially in evaluating how well students have developed the skills of inquiring. Yet this approach can also be quite frustrating to students unaccustomed to learning on their own. Therefore, until students develop frames of reference and concepts that give birth to effective questions and until they become familiar with inquiry itself, we need to guide and assist them in learning by asking questions and by stimulating them to ask relevant questions.

Another way we might organize such an experience is to allow the students to define a problem for investigation and then to guide the inquiry ourselves. Rather than feed data, we should encourage students to ask questions which when countered with questions requiring them to engage in intellectual operations, develop the answers to their original questions. Thus, to a question such as, "Why do these people select a leader that way?" we might respond by asking, "Why do you think?" In this way we can very subtly guide the students into the beginning of an inquiry experience.

There is yet another way of organizing questioning that is much more direct. We may supply a problematic situation and, after the students have articulated the problem, ask them directly to hypothesize some alternative solutions. Then, by using the types of questions outlined above, we may guide them through the various stages of intellectual inquiry from identifying the kinds of evidence needed to developing meaningful conclusions and even generalizing. Whereas in the previous approach the initiative is left mostly to the students, here it lies almost wholly in the hands of the teacher.

Which of these approaches to use depends on the objectives set for or by the students and their individual skills and backgrounds. If the objective is to test student abilities to use the skills of inquiring, then the nondirective approach may be most useful. If it is to learn how to ask questions and what questions to ask when, then the second approach is best. Or if it is to learn the process of inquiring and to learn some predetermined concept or generalization, a more directive approach may be advisable.

Regardless of the approach used, it is important to realize that inquiring proceeds at different rates of speed for different students, depending upon the varying intellectual abilities of the students, their backgrounds of experience, and the data with which they are working. Questions may come directly from the teacher as the entire class works through a teacher-directed activity. These questions may be asked orally or appear in the form of a study guide for use by small groups or individuals engaged in independent study; these guides may be written or typed or on filmstrips, depending on the nature of the material. For those unacquainted with this way of learning, these questions may be numerous and explicit; for the more experienced they may be fewer in number and less detailed. But no matter by which media they are communicated, questions must be carefully devised and presented in a sequence designed to get the student to proceed through all the various stages of rational inquiry.

The Role of Content

Another essential element of inquiry teaching is content. Inquiry does not occur in a vacuum. It requires something to work with, to inquire into, to think about. A certain amount of content or data is required to generate a problem, arouse curiosity, or create a question in the minds of the students. Additional content is needed to generate tentative solutions or answers. Even more content is needed to test hypotheses. If one hypothesis proves invalid, the entire experience becomes part of the data on which to hypothesize anew, and the process repeats. If a hypothesis appears to be substantiated by the data, then the resulting conclusion may be considered as data itself—though somewhat tentative—and held until it is applied to new but similar content. Data, or content, is plugged into and used at virtually every stage of inquiry teaching.

The type of content that may be used is unlimited. It may be lists of kings or presidents, information about laws passed during Reconstruction, data about a particular ethnic group in Africa, or a description of a trial. It may be on any subject or from any discipline. One most useful form of data is raw, primary data—statistics, maps, artifacts, paintings, pictures, diaries, documents, eyewitness accounts, poems, novels, and so on—data unaccompanied by explanations of what it says, what it means, why it is significant, or how it is related to something else. Textbook accounts, newspaper editorials or features, monographs, interpretive films, reports, and similar secondary materials may also be useful even though they usually represent what someone else believes to be true. As long as content is treated as data and not final answers, any kind of content may be used in inquiry teaching. Secondary accounts may be used as foils to motivate lessons, as sounding boards against which to check the results of student inquiry, as evaluative devices ("In view of our study, how valid is this interpretation?"), as sources of data, or as materials to be analyzed in terms of bias, methodology, and so on. Primary accounts may be used for similar purposes as well as to check the accuracy or authenticity of secondary accounts.

Although the kinds of content that are useful in inquiry teaching are basically no different from those often used in expository teaching, the role of this content is quite different. In expository teaching content tends to be an end in itself. Remembering it is usually the sole learning objective. In inquiry teaching, content is not an end in itself; it is not to be memorized. Its absorption is not the major objective of the learning experience. Instead, content is a vehicle for accomplishing something else—for clarifying values perhaps, or developing concepts and generalizations, or refining the skills of intellectual inquiry. It is used, manipulated, pulled apart, and refitted into new patterns in an effort to develop new meanings relevant to the task at hand. The major role of content in inquiry teaching is to serve as a vehicle for learning something else.

Content may also be used to guide the learning process. The kinds of information with which students are put in touch and the times at which this data is received influence how as well as what they learn. So too does the way in which the data is organized. If, for example, students deal only with data that implies an economic basis for imperialism, they will probably develop an economic explanation for it. If they are then put in touch with data that refutes or casts doubt on the validity of this explanation, they may ask new questions and search out new kinds of data to investigate. Thus, the way in which content is made available to students and how it is organized may be used to guide them in learning.

There are a number of reasons for controlling student access to content in inquiry teaching, at least in its initial stages. One is merely to save time. There is no reason why students should have to find their own data other than to develop the skills of finding relevant information. But this is only one set of skills necessary to learning. Time must be spent in refining the others too. Hence, we should frequently supply the students with the data they need so that what little time is available may be devoted to practicing these other skills. Moreover, great masses of content may overwhelm students unfamiliar with how to work with it. In this instance, too, we should provide it to them slowly and in usable amounts. In many cases also the kinds of content needed by the students may be inaccessible to them, so we should collect it and give it to them. Because inquiry teaching is much more than finding information, attention must be devoted to developing all inquiry skills, not just one.

Content may be highly structured or totally unstructured. All data dealing with government, for example, might be grouped in one section while all that on geography might be grouped in another. By helping students note similarities and differences such grouping directs them in the development of discipline-oriented concepts. While forming such concepts is often desirable, having students sometimes work with completely unorganized content is just as desirable for they can use what concepts they are evolving to order the data in their own fashion. Using content arranged in different ways helps students refine the skills of analysis and broaden analytical concepts—important objectives of inquiry teaching.

This is not to say that some content is not worth knowing or that learning content cannot be an objective of inquiry teaching. There is considerable content in the social studies that students should learn, and there is every indication that they can learn it well through inquiry teaching. Because inquiry-oriented learning experiences require students to talk about, mentally manipulate, and even physically work with information or content over and over again, students become so familiar with this content that they know it in the deepest sense of "knowing." They don't memorize it. It just becomes a part of their experience because they use it. In so doing, however, they learn other things as well.

Learning Materials

Content, as has already been noted, may be communicated through a variety of media. One of the most commonly used media in social studies seems to be the written word. Even the materials used in inquiry teaching often consist almost exclusively of collections of documents, other written sources, or excerpts therefrom. This is highly unfortunate and most undesirable.

One reason why a great many students find social studies courses boring or difficult is the frequently excessive amount of reading which they are required to do as well as the poor quality of most of the writing they must read. Students need to learn how to read, of course, and one way to help them accomplish this is to use text or documentary materials. But not exclusively. Students also need to work with other types of media, especially those which they will have opportunities to use in their out-of-school lives. It is vitally important in inquiry teaching that students gain experience in using a wide variety of media other than books and documents.

Lectures, oral reports, guest speakers, debates, songs, newspapers, novels, film loops, sound films, statistics, maps, records, tapes, television programs, and punch cards are just a few of the non-text media useful in learning. Each of these has special attributes. Maps and aerial photographs, for example, depict spatial distributions and areal relationships better than any other media; overhead transparencies are ideally suited to clarifying relationships and sequence. Content should be communicated through whatever media best reveals what is to be shown. And especially in inquiry teaching, the same content ought to be presented via a number of different media—for example, via a map and a chart or graph as well as a photograph—so that students may develop a variety of insights about its significance.

However, inquiry teaching can be employed effectively without access to all or most of the equipment or materials associated with the media described above. Even though many teachers who feel their instructional resources are limited to only a single, standard text claim that inquiry teaching is impossible for them, nothing is farther from the truth. No teacher is limited to a single text no matter how bleak the situation may appear.

Every classroom teacher, regardless of grade level or school facilities, has a number of potential resources which can serve as media for inquiry teaching. First, there are the public communications media—television, radio, and movies—at least one of which is readily accessible to almost everyone. Second, there are the students, each of whom possesses a rich and unique background of prior experience. Third, there is the teacher himself—his knowledge, talents, and interests, all of which can be used to enhance learning in the classroom. (A teacher can, for instance, make many of his own materials by taking photographs and slides, using cleared X-ray film on which to draw maps for overlays, and so on.) All of these resources can be tapped at various stages in any inquiry-teaching experience to identify problems worthy of investigation, to stimulate and suggest hypotheses, alternative plans of attack, and potential consequences of specific decisions, to provide data for testing hypotheses, and to serve as a basis for synthesizing a line of inquiry.

Finally, there is the textbook itself. A traditional social studies text can be well used as a basis for inquiry teaching. Any average textbook, especially those produced since 1965 or so, are really much more than collections of words. In addition to the written text, they usually contain all kinds of other learning aids including maps, graphs, charts, cartoons, photographs, timelines, and end-of-chapter word lists and questions. Many texts today, in fact, are simply multimedia packages bound with hard covers.

There are many ways in which a standard text may be used in inquiry teaching. The study of a unit or chapter can be launched, for example, by having the students examine the list of "Words to Define" that customarily follows a chapter or unit (and which is normally assigned after the chapter is read), much like the way a list of words has been used to launch our study of the Hausa. The students might look at these words, use dictionaries to define those which are unfamiliar, and then hypothesize characteristics of the period or subject presented in the chapter. They can then proceed to study the chapter to see if their hypotheses are indeed correct. Any photographs or other visual aids in a chapter may be used in the same way.

Another way to use a standard text in inquiry teaching is to identify generalizations made by the authors or statements expressing their points of view about something and then, treating these as hypotheses, analyze the content in the text relevant to these in order to test their validity. Still another approach might be to examine the graphic or map data included in a chapter in order to postulate ideas about issues or trends in the period to be studied and then examine the chapter to secure evidence against which to test these hypotheses. A chapter title, introduction, or summary might also be used in this manner.

There are additional approaches that may be used by teachers who have access to a number of traditional texts by different authors and publishers (such as the old sample copies which so often clutter schoolroom bookshelves). Students may each read paragraphs or sections on the same topic in different books and then compare the data and points of view presented for accuracy, bias, and scholarship as well as for more content-oriented objectives. Students may also evaluate positions or data presented by one text in terms of the information presented in others.

A traditional textbook can be quite effectively used in inquiry teaching, but such use requires teachers to change the way in which they are accustomed to using texts. A teacher cannot, for example, start at page one, proceed to page two, and move progressively, page-by-page or chapter-by-chapter, through the book. He must be willing to skip around, even within a chapter. Nor can a teacher be satisfied with having his students start with the introduction of a chapter and read through to the end. He must be willing sometimes to start with the word list at the end, the pictures or graphs in the chapter, or just an isolated statement. Finally, the teacher must be willing to encourage students to use the book actively while engaged in the learning experience. Rather than talking about facts they may or may not remember, learners should have the opportunity to thumb through pages to find the data necessary to make a point or test a hypothesis. As long as a text is seen as a compendium of information to be absorbed or memorized, it cannot be very useful in inquiry teaching. When it is viewed as a tool or a collection of various kinds of resources to be used for other purposes, however, a traditional social studies text can actually be very valuable to inquiry teaching.

Any type of learning material can be useful in inquiry teaching. Technical qualities aside, there is no such thing as a bad piece of material in this type of teaching. Some materials, of course, may be inferior or inadequate in the technical sense—that is, the sound may be fuzzy, the paper easily torn, the ink faded, the photographs blurred or too small, and so on. But whether or not the content of a piece of material is good or bad depends not on its accuracy, thoroughness, or bias but on how we use it. If we use a piece of material having inaccurate content as something to be committed unquestioningly to memory, then it is this use of it which is bad. This same piece of material might serve a very good purpose if we use it to raise questions, generate hypotheses, challenge assumptions, or evaluate student-made conclusions. How we use materials in inquiry teaching and not the nature of their content determines their value. There are no learning materials that cannnot be well used in some aspect of inquiry teaching.

Involvement of Students

Inquiry teaching differs from the more traditional expository teaching in another important aspect. Inquiry teaching requires the active involvement of the student in the learning experience. Since this type of teaching strategy does not consist solely of passing on to students the results of someone else's wit and wisdom, students cannot remain passive absorbers of information. They must become active seekers. They find problems to investigate, search for tentative answers, use data to validate hypotheses, synthesize content into new meanings, and perhaps even apply it in new situations. Inquiry is making meaning, and this is the job of learners not teachers. Inquiry teaching is designed to help students make meaning. It requires them to engage in the very process they are learning. Student interaction—with content and with each other—is an important characteristic of inquiry teaching.

Inquiry-learning experiences must thus be designed to facilitate this interaction and intellectual activity. Large-group classes—whether they include thirty or three hundred students—cannot be a mainstay of inquiry teaching. Students must instead spend considerable time in small-group discussion or individual study, research, and investigation. Of course, there are times when large-group sessions may be most useful such as when introducing a new subject for study or presenting hard-to-find data that all will need or evaluating the results of a learning experience. But by and large the bulk of class time must be organized so as to enable students to interact with each other as well as with the teacher, book, film, picture, or other media being used. Students can work in small groups or committees or as individuals. In inquiry teaching, students must spend less time in large-group situations than they normally do in traditional social studies instruction and more time in small groups or in independent inquiry.

The implications of group size should be quite clear. Large-group–small-group scheduling practices may not be at all conducive to inquiry teaching simply because these practices often lack the flexibility needed to allow for individualized inquiry or grouping or pairing. Instead of structuring teaching by prescribing a certain class size to meet at a certain interval each week, inquiry teaching must be organized on the basis of the kinds of intellectual activities that are involved in learning. Although the general stages are always the same, the time devoted to each depends on the topics under investigation, the students, and the learning objectives. These vary considerably.

Inquiry teaching can best be undertaken within an average-size class. Having the students regularly in one room enables the teacher to organize them as the situation warrants. They may sit as an entire class to view a film or hear a presentation; they may be paired with their neighbors in order to evaluate some data and form a hypothesis; they may be arranged in small groups within the room to test certain aspects of the hypothesis against specific evidence; they may go individually to the library or study center to gather more evidence; and they may reconvene periodically as a whole to report to each other, discuss problems, and debate conclusions. Successful inquiry teaching requires that students be deployed in a variety of ways designed to enhance their interaction with each other and with the data being used. The average classroom of twenty or thirty or forty students offers the flexibility needed for this arrangement.

Importance of Variety

Variety is just as important in inquiry teaching as in any other type of teaching. Perhaps more so. Any kind of teaching can become deadly monotonous if the same pattern is followed without alteration. But inquiry teaching more than expository teaching requires considerable intellectual effort. Hence, students need variety for at least two reasons—for a change of pace and to develop fully all the skills of inquiry that should be developed. This variety does not mean just the periodic introduction of a film or a field trip, however. It means varying the techniques, the materials, and the sequence of steps in the teaching strategy itself.

A considerable number of different instructional media and techniques should be used throughout any inquiry-teaching course or unit. The basic stages of inquiring provide the unifying threads for such an experience, but different techniques may be used in each. For example, the first problem might be presented by use of some quotations and pictures. The next problematic situation might be developed by use of newspaper accounts, the next by a role-playing activity, the next by contradictory quotations, the next by a sound film, and so on. Students may hypothesize in a general class discussion or in small groups. Hypotheses might be tested by all students using all the data or by different groups testing selected aspects of a hypothesis.

Each inquiry experience should be fresh in terms of the media used. By employing a multimedia approach, the teacher can help students refine their skills of using a wider variety of media as well as many of those they may expect to find relevant in out-of-school life. And the teacher should get into the habit of using the media best suited to the purpose. When he feels it necessary to present data, he may do it one time via film, another time by a record, later by a lecture, and even later by a set of still pictures. Homework assignments may include reading, analyzing maps or charts, studying photographs, and so on. There is nothing more deadening than beginning each unit with the same kind of technique or media, then hypothesizing with the same kind of media and/or technique, and so on.

Variety may also be ensured by changing the ways in which students are arranged for the various stages of inquiring. If in one unit they hypothesize as a class, in the next they might do it in pairs. If in one unit hypothesizing is done in the classroom, in another it might be a homework assignment. Techniques to be used, media to be employed, and the way students are organized are quite interrelated. Any combination of these should be determined according to how well it will accomplish the desired objectives. Since there are many skill, attitude, and knowledge objectives which ought to be sought in inquiry teaching, these combinations should vary greatly throughout the overall learning experience.

Varying inquiry teaching does not end here, however. The strategy itself may be varied not only to avoid monotony but also to concentrate on specific sets of skills associated with particular parts of the strategy. Although inquiring normally begins with developing a problem, the students do not have to begin each unit this way, for if they do, they will not be long in realizing that if they fail to come up with a problem, they will not have to proceed further; or if they choose a ridiculous problem, they may destroy whatever the teacher has planned; or if they argue long enough, they won't have time for anything else.

To avoid these situations and at the same time to get maximum use out of what little time is available, we may sometimes give the students a problem or present one for study which has been a subject of concern to many people. Or we can skip this phase of inquiry altogether and introduce the students to a theory or hypothesis advanced by some scholar, for instance, and ask them to determine how well the available data supports it. Such a theory then becomes the problem and eliminates the need to develop a student-initiated problem. A learning experience might even be launched by looking at the evidence that someone else has used to verify his own hypothesis. In the process of analyzing this, students may not only find new evidence but also refine their skills of working with data.

Variety is important for pedagogical as well as for psychological or humanitarian reasons. Fresh approaches are more exciting and interesting. Doing the same old thing with the same media the same way for every learning experience is stifling to say the least. This is as true for inquiry teaching as it is for any other kind of teaching. Ensuring that this monotony does not occur is an important aspect of inquiry teaching.

The Role of
the Teacher

Classroom teachers play a more important role in inquiry teaching than in any other kind of teaching. Whether or not inquiry occurs in the classroom is entirely in our hands. To be successful, we must know what inquiry is and how to go about it; we must be inquirers ourselves. We must practice what we preach and be able to organize and facilitate learning experiences that require students to engage in intellectual inquiry.

The primary function of any teaching is to facilitate learning—to stimulate it, to guide it, and to ensure that it happens. Doing this is our responsibility. In expository teaching we generally fulfill this responsibility by telling students what they ought to learn. In inquiry teaching, however, we facilitate learning by the instructional techniques we use and the ways in which we arrange them, by the content we select and the way in which we structure it, by the classroom climate we create, and by the role we take in the actual learning experience. The degree to which inquiry teaching is successful depends largely on our abilities to accomplish these things.

Effective inquiry teaching requires us to function on two distinct levels—as planners and as facilitators of learning. We must first design the course: its component units, the individual learning experiences which comprise these units, and when necessary, the instructional materials that will be used in them. Then we must translate these from paper to an actual classroom setting by bringing about the behaviors we have determined will best achieve the objectives that have been established.

Plannning for Inquiry Teaching .

Advanced planning for inquiry teaching is absolutely essential. This planning involves establishing the desired objectives, selecting appropriate content, and then selecting and arranging in sequence the activities which will help the students:

1. Define problems for investigation.
2. Hypothesize—develop tentative answers, alternative solutions, or possible plans of attack.
3. Test these against evidence.
4. Draw meaningful conclusions about the validity of the hypothesis.
5. Either continue hypothesizing and testing each succeeding hypothesis until a valid "answer" is developed or, having arrived at such a conclusion, apply it to new data.
6. Generalize or conceptualize on the basis of the entire learning experience.

Such planning means conducting what is, in a sense, an imaginary dry run through the contemplated learning experience. In doing so, we must anticipate the kinds of hypotheses that may be offered, identify the data and materials that may be needed to test these, and speculate about the kinds of questions that may be raised or may need to be raised. This planning is absolutely essential to an effective classroom learning experience because only in this way can we determine the kinds of content and media that will probably be needed or work best in the course of the planned learning experience. Only in this way is it possible to devise the proper questions and to arrange the various learning activities in a sequence that will help the learner move from the initiatory problem to its resolution.

Our main concern in planning as in conducting the actual classroom experience must be how best to guide learning toward the predetermined objectives. Several of the tools that we use to guide learning must be developed in this planning stage. These include the questions that are to be asked and the data or content that is to be used.

In selecting questions to ask or be asked, we must be aware of the fact that what one learns and how one learns are determined in part by the kinds of questions asked, the order in which they are asked, and when they are asked. In planning an inquiry-teaching experience we need to select questions that will require students to hypothesize, questions that will require them to identify the evidence needed to test the hypothesis, and questions that will require them to arrange and analyze this evidence in productive fashion. There are many kinds of such questions, but there is only one way they can be arranged—so that they stimulate the students to move through the process of and use the skills of intellectual inquiry.

The same may be said of content and of the media by which it is communicated. What one learns and how one learns is determined in part by the kinds of data used, the order in which it is used, and when it becomes available. By withholding data representing contradictory views on a particular issue or event, we may actually allow students to reach questionable conclusions. By then making this data available, we can lead them to evaluate their inquiry. By presenting only workable amounts of data at a time, we may focus on the development of different skills rather than overwhelm the students with an avalanche of content.

In many instances the kinds of materials needed for a particular learning experience are not available or at least are unavailable in a form commensurate with the abilities of the students. Consequently, we must prepare the materials ourselves. This is another important part of planning. Maps often need to be collected, redrawn, or created; transparencies need to be prepared; charts need to be typed or drawn. In order to conduct a worthwhile inquiry-learning experience, the proper materials must be available, and selecting or making these must be done before the actual learning experience is launched.

Making decisions about content, media, and questions—which to use, how to arrange them, and when to do what—are the very essence of designing inquiry-learning experiences. Only by carefully advanced and detailed planning can a worthwhile learning experience be created. Such planning is the sine qua non of inquiry teaching.

Conducting the Learning Experience

There are other ways in which we may guide an inquiry experience, too. But while these ways may to some degree be planned in advance, they are basically the product of how we operate in our classrooms. This involves the second facet of facilitating learning—conducting the learning experience.

A classroom climate conducive to free and open intellectual inquiry is essential to inquiry teaching. Such a climate is one in which students are free to question and discuss, to communicate with each other as well as with the teacher and other media, to direct the learning experience into areas of their interests, and to consider their reasoned views as legitimate as those of anyone else.

Of course, such a climate is partially the result of the equipment in the classroom and how it is arranged. A room with movable student desks and chairs, with numerous written, audio, and visual references and resources, and with readily available materials is indispensable. But another factor which affects the learning climate in a classroom is our own behavior as teachers.

A climate conducive to inquiry is not created by our standing behind a lectern at the front of the room while students are required to stand when reciting. It is created by designing challenging problems to resolve, by using techniques (such as pairing and grouping) that foster student interaction and minimize our intervention and domination, and by our enthusiastically joining the students as an inquirer. It is not created by our giving answers or by determining the validity of an answer by a show of hands ("How many agree with John?") or by requiring students to guess what answer we are looking for or by requiring all students to come up with the same answer or even by talking in terms of a preconceived right answer. A climate conducive to inquiry demands that we redirect questions to the students, new questions, and give the students an opportunity to find out for themselves.

An inquiring climate is not created, moreover, by demanding silence throughout the entire class period. It is created by realizing that silence is not always golden and by permitting and even encouraging students to talk among themselves before they venture opinions, hypotheses, and the like. It is not created by repeating the same question in different forms when no response is immediately forthcoming. It is created by allowing time for questions to sink in, for students to think about them and even talk about them. It is brought about by using the lesson plan to get the lesson going, by building on student input, and by referring thereafter to the plan only for the most basic guidance.

A classroom climate conducive to inquiry is not created by keeping the students arranged forever in neat little rows but by encouraging—indeed, even requiring—them to move into groups and pairs to engage in some aspect of inquiry. It is not brought about by requiring silence when viewing some visual material and then by urging discussion of what everyone thinks they saw or heard, but it is created by showing and reshowing the film or filmstrip and by talking about it while it is being shown. An inquiry climate is not created by ignoring unanticipated contributions or questions but by treating the contributions of all students with the respect that thinking deserves.

Effective inquiry teaching requires considerable awareness of the fact that what we say and do affects how students learn as well as what they learn. Students whose contributions receive a "That's right!" response from us are in reality being rewarded by an outsider when in fact they should be getting these rewards from inside—from knowing their contributions are right because the data supports them. Students who get enough "That's wrong!" responses eventually stop contributing altogether. Such a situation is hardly conducive to learning.

We must avoid putting students down and thus turning them away from further thinking. We must also avoid ignoring obviously invalid statements or ridiculing them or responding with an "uh huh" or "that's interesting" or some other noncommittal remark. We may challenge these contributions or ask others to comment on them, but we should never ignore or try to sidestep them. Neither should we write on the board only the ideas we want and ignore any others, because in so doing, we are really indicating to the contributors whether or not we think their ideas count.

Instead, we must reward all results of thinking by accepting the contributions and using them in the learning experience. All answers ought to be treated as hypotheses subject to later verification. And evidence should be required. A snap answer of "Charlemagne" to the question "Who won the battle of Saratoga?" should not be dismissed as inane but rather accepted as a hypothesis and tested by reference to other data. The data should tell if it is invalid—not the teacher.

Above all, we should require students to do the summarizing or concluding. We should avoid ending a class by saying "Well, today we learned. . . ." How do we know what was learned? Only the students can tell—either verbally or by some other observable behavior—what they have learned.

As teachers, in conducting inquiry, we thus have many roles. We must, for one thing, facilitate communication. We must require students to define their terms and help them say as precisely as possible what they mean. We must see to it that all students get involved and that students talk to each other rather than only to us. Secondly, we must promote thinking. This requires us to guide the students through the process of inquiry, stopping periodically so that they may summarize what has been established to that point. In so doing, we may have to correct errors in fact or even challenge questionable statements. Sometimes we will have to supply hard-to-get data or steer students to sources of information we know will be useful to them. We may have to act as a devil's advocate by asking questions or injecting data that directly contradicts what the students are saying. We may have to prod or slow students down. We may have to help unsnarl confusion or ambiguity. And we may have to help the students step back and reexamine what they have been doing. At times we will even have to help the students make connections between what they have learned and what they are now doing.

Successful execution of these roles requires us to be models for inquiry. We must not only know how to inquire—we must do it with enthusiasm. We must not in any way be authoritarian or dogmatic. We must be most flexible in our teaching techniques. We must permit and encourage challenging questions and creative thinking. We must not insist that what we believe to be true is true but rather must accept all views and interpretations for submission to the test of the evidence. And we must do the same for our own views.

We must also continually evaluate what is happening in the course of our planned learning experience. We must learn to know when the students have successfully attained each step in the inquiry process as well as when they have learned what we want them to know. This evaluation may be based on observation as well as on written evidence. Of course paper and pencil tests may also be administered. The point is that evaluation must be an ongoing effort if the inquiry teaching experience is to lead anywhere because we cannot possibly guide the class to a new level of thinking unless they have attained the preceding level.

Although inquiry teaching often makes some people feel insecure, it should not. The security of good inquiry teaching lies more in knowing how to inquire than it does in any specific body of content. To achieve this security, we must know the process of inquiring, be well organized, be adept at using the skills of inquiry, and have a conceptual framework that leads us to ask a wide variety of useful questions. Security in the classroom lies in knowing what to do next, in knowing that if we just formulated a hypothesis, the next thing to do is identify the kinds of data we need to verify it; or in knowing that if we are working with data, we must translate, classify, and interpret it. Knowledge of how to inquire and willingness to engage in inquiry are basic attributes of successful and confident inquiry teachers.

Not all teachers may be able to fill these roles. Or at least not all may be comfortable in so doing. Inquiry teaching requires flexibility, considerable tolerance for ambiguity, a willingness to say "I don't know," a refusal to give answers, and a knowledge of how to inquire. It also requires considerable knowledge of the content and of the skills being used. It demands an open, creative, enthusiastic person, and not all of us have these attributes.

Evaluating the Learning Experience

Evaluation properly conceived is more than confronting students with a ten-question, class-opening quiz or a fifty-item test at the conclusion of each unit. Evaluation is an ongoing process. It occurs throughout the learning experience as we try to determine whether or not the students have reached a certain stage in the learning process so they can profitably proceed to the next stage. We actually evaluate constantly—sometimes by observation, other times by questioning. In each instance we look for some indication that what we have been doing or seeking is sufficiently clear to the students. This is one reason why a rather detailed lesson plan is so useful. Having thought out and noted the key learning operations in which we wish the students to engage and the things they will say or do to indicate they are ready to undertake such operations, then our on-the-spot evaluation need not be a hit-or-miss affair and our teaching will be that much more effective. Good evaluation requires continuous effort. It is essential to the effectiveness of any teaching strategy.

Evaluating the results of inquiry teaching too often appears to be much more difficult than it is, however. Successful measurement of this type of instruction requires basically just two things. First, we must distinguish between the various types of objectives for which inquiry teaching may be used. And second, we must understand that if we wish to discover what students know, what they can do, or how they feel about something, we may ask them either to tell directly or to demonstrate it otherwise.

There are a variety of instructional objectives for which inquiry teaching may be used. These include knowledge of facts, concepts, and generalizations, knowledge of thinking and study skills, and possession of certain attitudes and values. If we define these objectives in terms of observable behaviors, then they can be adequately measured. The degree to which each of these objectives is attained as a result of a particular learning experience may be evaluated in different ways.

Knowledge objectives of inquiry teaching may be classified either as substantive (factual or conceptual knowledge) or process (skill) objectives. If we wish to determine just how well a student knows a certain skill, we can ask him to tell us orally or in an essay how he would go about using that skill. Or, better yet, we can put him in a testing situation where he must use the skill in order to answer a question. It is quite possible, for example, to devise multiple choice and other objective questions to evaluate how well students can use, and thus presumably know, the skills of rational thinking. Such questions really correspond to the final stage of inquiry teaching—applying knowledge to new data.

Questions designed to evaluate knowledge of skills generally consist of two parts: first, some type of data for the students to work with and second, a series of questions about this data which require students to engage in certain intellectual operations with this data in order to arrive at acceptable answers. The data that is provided must be unfamiliar to the students. If it is not, if the students have previously studied this data in class, any questions about it will likely only test the students' ability to recall previous answers rather than their ability to use certain skills. Consequently, the data given on the test must be new to the students. It may be presented in any number of forms—as a map, a graph or chart, a paragraph, a conversation, a cartoon, and so on—depending on the type of skills to be evaluated.

The questions accompanying the given data may test a variety of skills. The first questions ought to be the simplest. They could, for instance, test the student's ability to translate only—to read what the given data literally says. Subsequent questions might then test the skills of interpreting—of telling what this data means. The following questions may serve to exemplify such inquiry tests of skill:

Africa's share of the world's output of selected minerals is shown on the following graph. Each △ represents 10% of the world's total output of the specified mineral:

Diamonds	△	△	△	△	△	△	△	△	△	◿
Cobalt Ore	△	△	△	△	△	△	△			
Gold	△	△	△	△	◿					
Copper	△	△	◿							
Chromite	△	△	◿							
Tin	△	◿								

1. Based on the above graph, what percentage of the world's supply of chromite is produced in Africa?

    a. 2½%
    b. 25%
    c. 50%
    d. 75%

2. Which of the following interpretations of this graph is most correct?

    a. Africa produces more diamonds than any other mineral.

    b. The production of gold is Africa's third greatest source of wealth.

    c. More copper is produced in Africa than chromite.

    d. Africa is a major producer of the world's supply of gold.

3. In the years following the discovery of a large supply of cobalt ore in Alaska and its production for world use, the number of symbols for cobalt on the above graph will probably:

    a. Increase

    b. Decrease

    c. Remain the same

    d. Disappear

Question one requires students only to translate what the graph says. Question two requires them to tell what the graph means—to interpret it. Question three requires them to go beyond the data—to extrapolate. If we want to find out if students could use the skills of synthesis, we could ask them to generalize about this data:

4. Which of the following conclusions can most accurately be supported by this graph?

    a. Africa is a major producer of several mineral resources.

    b. Africa produces most of the world's mineral resources.

    c. Mineral production is Africa's greatest source of wealth.

    d. Producing minerals is a major part of Africa's economy.

Questions designed to test the students' ability to use other skills may also be added. A number of questions structured such as these and requiring students to translate data, interpret it, synthesize it, and so on may be used on any test if the intent is to evaluate how well students know specific inquiry skills.

The same techniques may be used to evaluate substantive knowledge—whether it be factual or conceptual. Students may be asked directly to recall or identify a certain fact ("How many independent nations are there in Latin America?") or a concept ("Describe the concept of revolution.") or a generalization ("What is the relationship between one's habitat and his way of life?"), and they may be expected to respond to these questions orally or in essays. Similar information may also be obtained through the use of objective questions such as multiple choice and matching items. For instance, we may offer different versions of a generalization about habitat and way of life, and then ask the students to choose the one best substantiated by the class study.

Another approach to assessing these same types of knowledge is to ask the students questions—objective or essay—which require them to apply what facts, concepts, or generalizations they know to new data. To evaluate students' knowledge of a concept of landscape, for instance, the teacher could ask them to examine a photograph of a local scene. To measure their knowledge of a concept of role, he could ask them to analyze the degree to which a certain person was successful in fulfilling a particular role. Such types of questions are quite sophisticated and require students to use what they know for a purpose. In essence, these questions require students to engage in the final stage of inquiring—applying a concept or generalization to new data to make it meaningful. The degree to which they discuss the content in terms of the various dimensions of the specified concept may serve as a measure of how well they know the concept.

One useful way to organize a paper and pencil test in inquiry teaching is to divide it into two parts: one part to evaluate substantive knowledge such as facts, definitions, concepts, and generalizations, and the other part to evaluate various inquiry skills. Use of such a test plan requires, of course, writing test items specially designed to measure the skills we wish to evaluate. For many of us, creating valid, reliable skill items is not easy and perhaps virtually impossible. Fortunately, however, there are model test items for inquiry skills that already exist.[19] All we need do is use these items as frameworks, and by changing the subject matter components, we can build questions to test any inquiry skill in any content area. Reference to these question models will prove invaluable to anyone engaged in evaluating substantive and skill knowledge in inquiry teaching.

Evaluating attitudes and values may take a similar approach. Students may be asked what they like or dislike or if they would be willing to do a certain thing. But answers to questions such as these are quite

[19] A ready-made source of model questions for use in evaluating cognitive (both content and skill) objectives is Benjamin Bloom et al., *Taxonomy of Educational Objectives—Handbook I: The Cognitive Domain* (New York: David McKay Co., 1956). A source of similar questions for use in evaluating affective objectives is David R. Krathwohl et al., *Taxonomy of Educational Objectives—Handbook II: The Affective Domain* (New York: David McKay Co., 1964). See also Dana Kurfman, "The Evaluation of Effective Thinking," in *Effective Thinking in the Social Studies,* eds. Jean Fair and Fannie R. Shaftel (Washington: National Council for the Social Studies, 1967), pp. 231–253; Bryon Massialas and Jack Zevin, *Creative Encounters in the Classroom* (New York: John Wiley & Sons, 1967); Edwin Fenton, *Teaching the New Social Studies in Secondary Schools: An Inductive Approach* (New York: Holt, Rinehart & Winston, 1966), pp. 283–298; and Norris Sanders, *Classroom Questions: What Kinds?* (New York: Harper & Row, 1966).

unreliable. A semantic differential or even preference tests are some-what more useful, especially if administered by a guidance counselor or some neutral party. But affective objectives may also be measured with even greater accuracy by observation.

How we feel about something is readily revealed by our behavior. If we dislike something, we do what we can to avoid it. We may even make disparaging remarks about it. Given a choice of coming in contact with it or avoiding it, we will consistently select the latter. If we like something, we may go out of our way to do it. We may buy books about it on our own. We may talk about it continually. We may even become a kind of expert on this "thing," a person our friends turn to when they need information about it or help with it. Observing be-haviors such as these should tell us if a person likes or dislikes a par-ticular thing. This is not as subjective as some would have us believe. If we can clearly define the types of behavior a student could exhibit to show us what he knows, what he can do, or how he feels about some-thing, recording and evaluating this behavior may be quite objective.

If a student brings us a clipping from a newspaper about a topic we have been studying, and he has never done this before; if he vol-unteers to make a report, answer a question, or find out something, and he has never done these things before; if he buys a paperback on our class topic when he could have spent his money in any number of other ways—he is very likely interested in what we are doing. Such behaviors may not be conclusive, but then neither are the results of many written tests.

Effective evaluation of inquiry teaching is a continous process. It is no more difficult than effective evaluation of any other kind of teaching. We may use a variety of techniques including paper and pencil testing, oral quizzing, and even observation. We may have the students tell us directly what they know or feel, or we may have them demon-strate their knowledge and feelings by working in unfamiliar situations or with unfamiliar data. Many evaluation models already exist to assist us in these efforts. We need only be aware that effective evaluation is as important to inquiry teaching as to all other teaching and that it requires considerable attention and effort.

The Role of
the Student

Just as our role in inquiry teaching differs from our role in the most traditional type of teaching, so too does the student's role. In ex-pository classrooms, the student is accustomed to sitting rather passively and, at best, soaking up what is said, reading what is assigned, and writing out answers to questions in the text—answers that can be found somewhere in the preceding chapter. He knows he is to remain quiet throughout the class period. He is to copy whatever we write on the board. His notebook is to be neat and up-to-date. Comparatively little intellectual effort is involved in these activities.

Students as a whole are well aware of how we expect them to act. And they act that way. They see themselves essentially as passive receivers to be acted upon by the teachers. They see the active role in learning as belonging to us. We do things to and for them. Students get out of the learning experience what we put into it!

In inquiry teaching, however, students get out of the learning experience what they put into it. Their role is one of making considerable intellectual effort—of working with information, initiating questions, challenging ideas, thinking. They may even do what they customarily assign to us—tell what they think is so or offer some information they have found. For many students, being confronted with this new set of expectations is quite difficult. As a result they do not take to this way of teaching until they become accustomed to the freedom and satisfaction it brings. For some, this never happens because they have too long derived satisfaction from being able to regurgitate the answers we want. When there are no particular right answers, these students feel lost. They are so programmed into the system that they find it almost impossible to succeed in inquiry teaching.

Such is particularly true of many students classified as honor students. Many of these students win this status because they are able to "read" us, guess what it is we want, and then do it. They are reluctant to ask questions—especially challenging questions—or introduce novel ideas because these might embarrass us or they might be "put down" as a result. Students in this category do not often get there by putting teachers on the spot. They memorize what they think is to be learned, and they do it well. They do not rush into contributing or answering questions until they are fairly sure they have the right answer because they do not care to appear wrong or foolish in front of their peers. Besides, they have a reputation to protect. An abrupt change to inquiry teaching may be most disconcerting for many students like this because it may require them to learn to use new skills and new reward systems.

But this is not so true of those frequently classified as below average students or underachievers. These students are, for the most part, ready and willing to engage actively in certain aspects of intellectual inquiry. They have no reputation to protect. They are rarely "right" anyway, so it is nothing new to them to offer a suggestion that may be "wrong." They are adept at hypothesizing—most of their answers in a traditional classroom are, in reality, hypotheses. Their major problem is in sustaining inquiry, but when they find that their conclusions can be as valid as anyone else's, they become most receptive to inquiry teaching.

Each kind of student often reacts the same way to inquiry-oriented teachers as they do to inquiry teaching. Students have a very definite image of what a teacher should do—give lectures, assign reading, ask factual questions based on the reading, know all the answers, and test to see if the content has been memorized. Exercises are graded. Audio-visual presentations may be "treats" or supplemental; they may be offered but rarely discussed and hardly ever considered essential to the unit under study. The teacher knows best and knows all. Students expect him to act in a certain way. When he doesn't, they question his competency or his interest in them. Many students of all ability levels still want to be told—for psychological security if for no other reason. Being confronted by inquiry teaching may be most upsetting and even frustrating to many of them.

Teachers need to be aware of these problems because much of the potential friction or frustration in initiating inquiry teaching can be avoided by treating students the way their new role demands. There is no teller-receiver, adult-child, teacher-client relationship. As Norman Johnson has noted, the student is more than a receiver, more than a child intellectually, more than a client.[20] To assume he is a receiver or a child or a client is to assume he has nothing to contribute to the learning experience. But on the contrary, every student can and does make input in any kind of learning experience. He does help initiate and direct these experiences, and he does have ideas as to what he ought and wants to do.

Students like all people will behave exactly as others expect them to behave. An effective inquiry teacher strives to help his students have a positive self-image, to help them realize they can think and succeed on their own. He does this by creating the kind of classroom climate for inquiry described above—by letting the test for truth be the evidence and the reward system the satisfaction of knowing "my idea is as good as anyone else's in view of the data." This is an important goal of all education and of inquiry teaching in particular.

Conclusion

Inquiry teaching is obviously not the only type of instructional strategy that can be used in the classroom. But it is the most useful strategy in which the main objective is conceptual—in which the primary purpose

---

[20] Norman Johnson, "The Problem As I See It," *Carnegie Review*, no.18 (February 1969): 11.

is to develop or refine a concept or generalization, to practice a skill of reflective thinking, or to develop or clarify an attitude or value about something. Inquiry teaching is not easy, but neither is it mysterious or impossible. It is, rather, a very precise way of teaching—one that, with continued practice, evaluation, and reflection, can be used by any good teacher. It is exciting for teacher and student alike. It is productive. And, it is fun.

What Next?

9

Inquiry teaching is not easy. Yet neither is any other type of good teaching. However, inquiry teaching is the most exciting, stimulating, and rewarding kind of teaching which one can undertake. There is considerably more to it than meets the eye at first glance. Inquiry teaching is a highly structured type of instructional strategy that is based on sound learning theory. Its great strength is that it makes learning a joint student-teacher quest for knowledge rather than a mere search for right answers. It can and does facilitate, better than any other type of teaching strategy, learning at all levels of knowledge while simultaneously helping to develop study skills, to refine intellectual skills of inquiry, and to clarify attitudes and values. It is, in sum, a way of teaching students how to learn by using the skills, processes, attitudes, and knowledge of rational thinking.

The intent of this volume has been to describe a concept of inquiry and a teaching strategy built on this concept. I have tried to develop the dimensions of this strategy slowly. If the ideas here have done nothing else, perhaps they have at least raised some questions about which we all should think a bit more deeply. Of course, it is extremely difficult to read about someone's else's perception of inquiry teaching and come away knowing about it in any great depth. To know about inquiry teaching requires considerable reflection about and actual classroom use of this teaching strategy. Inquiry teaching is not something that can be picked up overnight and used immediately with perfect success. It requires a great deal of time and work to become adept at it and to be comfortable with it. For those who may wish to find out more about this teaching strategy and eventually to try it in their own classrooms, perhaps some of the following suggestions may be useful.

1. Although it was not my original intent to deal with a rationale for using inquiry teaching in the social studies classroom, two superb books on this topic have recently been published which are *must* reading for anyone interested in inquiry. Both are extremely well written, provocative, and stimulating. Before even considering how to initiate or improve inquiry teaching in your classroom, read, study, and discuss with your colleagues:

Kellum, David. *The Social Studies—Myths and Realities.* New York: Sheed and Ward, 1969.

This book is the most exciting, challenging, and provocative book on social studies teaching in print. Kellum deals with numerous traditional aspects, challenging most of them and raising embarrassing and relevant questions about each. Reflection on his ideas on history, motivation, testing, curriculum, teaching styles, and minority groups will provide a fine basis for a personal rationale for inquiry teaching in social studies.

Postman, Neil, and Weingartner, Charles. *Teaching as a Subversive Activity.* New York: The Delacorte Press, 1969.

If Kellum's book doesn't provide a cogent argument for using inquiry in social studies, this one will. The insights to be gained from these authors about the use (and misuse) of language, the nature of meaning-making, relevant knowledge, motivation, and the like are invaluable for anyone planning to engage in inquiry teaching in social studies at any grade level.

2. Examine and analyze—with others of like mind—some good examples of inquiry in action, such as those contained in:

Massialas, Byron, and Zevin, Jack. *Creative Encounters in the Classroom.* New York: John Wiley & Sons, 1969.

This is essentially a discussion of inquiry learning and teaching using transcripts of classroom dialogue to illustrate certain aspects of discovery. Samples of lessons include activities in geography, "non-Western" studies, history, and values (pp. 73–164, 187–193, and 215–246). Examination of these and the authors' analyses of them may provide useful insights into how to go about planning for inquiry teaching.

Fenton, Edwin, ed. *Teaching the New Social Studies in Secondary Schools: An Inductive Approach.* New York: Holt, Rinehart & Winston, 1966.

This volume includes an excellent sample of classroom dialogue on pages 264–274 in which students conceptualize about a number of ideas. The teacher's lesson plan for this lesson is reproduced on pages 177–179. Examination of these will provide insight into ways in which inquiry teaching may become a classroom reality.

3. Study some of the better monographs on inquiry learning and/or inquiry teaching, such as:

Allen, Rodney, et al., eds. *Inquiry in the Social Studies.* Washington: National Council for the Social Studies, 1968.

This collection of short essays and articles gleaned largely from the professional literature focuses especially on various models of inquiry as well as on questions and structure. It also includes transcripts of several classroom discussions and model learning materials.

Fair, Jean, and Shaftel, Fannie R., eds. *Effective Thinking in the Social Studies.* 37th Yearbook. Washington: National Council for the Social Studies, 1967.

The most relevant segments of this volume are the chapters by Charlotte Crabtree on reflective thinking, Millard Clements on inquiry as related to various disciplines, and Hilda Taba on thinking. Dana Kurfman's chapter on evaluating thinking is excellent.

Massialas, Byron, and Cox, C. Benjamin. *Inquiry in Social Studies.* New York: McGraw-Hill Book Co., 1966.

This volume is a scholarly analysis of the nature and use of inquiry in the social studies classroom. It focuses especially on the theoretical rationale for inquiry as well as on participation techniques, evaluation procedures, and materials.

4. Analyze and refer continuously to readable and practical descriptions of how to organize and conduct inquiry teaching and learning experiences, such as:

Lippitt, Ronald; Fox, Robert; and Schaible, Lucille. *The Teacher's Role in Social Science Investigation.* Chicago: Science Research Associates, 1969.

Originally designed as a guide to a new elementary social studies program, this book contains excellent practical descriptions of and suggestions for using techniques of value inquiry, data collection, and analysis, for making and interpreting questionnaires, for intra-class grouping, and for evaluation in the classroom. The ideas are applicable to all grade levels.

Hunt, Maurice P., and Metcalf, Lawrence. *Teaching High School Social Studies.* 2d ed. New York: Harper & Row, Publishers, 1968.

A classic social studies "methods" text on teaching for reflective thinking, this book devotes pages 65–274 to the teaching of concepts, generalizations, and value analysis. Attention is also given to motivation, discussion, and evaluation techniques.

Raths, Louis, et al. *Teaching for Thinking: Theory and Application.* Columbus, Ohio: Charles E. Merrill Books, 1967.

This book describes a theory of instruction for teaching children how to think. It also provides numerous examples of lessons and learning experiences which teachers may use to help students learn how to observe, summarize, compare, classify, and interpret.

Sanders, Norris. *Classroom Questions: What Kinds?* New York: Harper & Row, Publishers, 1966.

This is an outline of questions organized according to types that may be used to elicit student thinking—translating data, interpreting data, analysis, synthesis, and evaluation. Reference to this volume will prove quite useful in designing inquiry-teaching lessons and evaluative devices.

Taba, Hilda. *Teacher's Handbook for Elementary Social Studies.* Palo Alto: Addison-Wesley Publishing Co., 1967.

This booklet is designed to introduce teachers to the Taba elementary social studies program. However, it is relevant to teaching social studies by inquiry at any grade level. Especially useful are the chapters containing guidelines for organizing inquiry-teaching lessons in the cognitive domain and on the types of questions most useful in this teaching.

5. Evaluate samples of inquiry-teaching lesson plans and instructional rationale, such as:

Fenton, Edwin, ed. *Teaching the New Social Studies in Secondary Schools: An Inductive Approach.* New York: Holt, Rinehart & Winston, 1966.

Fenton's book contains numerous examples of inquiry-oriented lessons and materials. Especially useful for analysis are the lessons outlined on pages 175–187 on how a historian works with data. Also useful are descriptions of various types of learning experiences in geography, political science, and other disciplines contained in pages 229–253 and 301–431.

Oliver, Donald, et al. *Cases and Controversy: Guide to Teaching* and *Supplement.* Columbus, Ohio: American Education Publications, 1967.

This teacher's guide to the Public Issues Series created by the Harvard Social Studies Project contains a rationale for this approach to social studies instruction as well as a description of the strategies it employs. It emphasizes the case studies approach to value clarification and appropriate discussion techniques. Teaching guides, tests, and sample classroom dialogues are included.

6. Analyze and evaluate outstanding examples of instructional materials (and the accompanying teacher guides) designed for use in inquiry teaching. Examination of each of the following materials, for example, will illustrate entirely different ways to use information about the coming of the American revolution in inquiry teaching.

Bennett, Peter S. *What Happened on Lexington Green: An Inquiry into the Nature and Methods of History.* Palo Alto: Addison-Wesley Publishing Co., 1969.

Kownslar, Allan O., and Frizzle, Donald B. *Discovering American History.* New York: Holt, Rinehart & Winston, 1967, pp. 97–128. Also available is a pamphlet, *Discovering American History: A Rationale.*

Oliver, Donald, and Newmann, Fred M. *The American Revolution.* Columbus, Ohio: American Education Publications, 1967. (For teacher's guide see pages 15–16 in *Cases and Controversy: Guide to Teaching.*)

One particular set of instructional materials deliberately attempts to teach and use the skills of inquiry as described in the preceding pages. These materials, with the general title of *African Images,* consist of a number of separate "mini-course" multi-media units, two of which may be especially useful at this point:

Beyer, Barry K., and Hicks, E. Perry. *Africa Inquiry Maps.* New York: Thomas Y. Crowell Co., 1970.

A set of 30 student map packages and a teaching guide designed to teach students how to use the skills of inquiry and a strategy for inquiring as they examine information about the peoples, products, topography, climate, and other features of Africa displayed on special transparent maps.

Beyer, Barry K., and Hicks, E. Perry. *Africans All*. New York: Thomas Y. Crowell Co., 1971.

A multimedia, "mini-course," learning program on the peoples and physical geography of Africa built directly on an inquiry-teaching strategy and designed to teach students how to use this strategy and its associated skills while they learn about Africans. The Hausa lessons and materials used in the preceding chapters are adapted from this program. An extensive teaching guide is included.

7. There are, of course, a host of other publications that might be of use in coming to grips with inquiry teaching. A number of films depicting classroom learning that are believed to exemplify various aspects of inquiry teaching might very well be examined in order to identify examples of various types of teacher and student behavior that one might find useful—or not useful—in inquiry teaching. Some films in this regard are:

How the Historian Classifies Information. New York: Holt, Rinehart & Winston, 1966. (16 mm, sound, b/w, 25 min.)

An inquiry-oriented learning experience involving a class grouping data in order to develop a concept.

The Medieval Cathedral: Using Picture Cards. New York: Holt, Rinehart & Winston, 1968. (16 mm, sound, b/w, 25 min.)

An inquiry-oriented learning experience involving the use of picture cards as an instructional media.

Teaching Public Issues. Middletown, Conn.: American Education Publications, 1969. (16 mm, sound, b/w)

Three films on techniques useful in value inquiry into public issues: *Developing a Position, Discussion Techniques,* and *Problems in Productive Discussion*

Day One and *Inference from Archeological Evidence*. Chicago: Anthropology Curriculum Study Project, 1969. (16 mm, sound, b/w)

Classes using materials from lessons devised by the Anthropology Curriculum Study Project involving uses of a site map to hypothesize about a particular people.

High School Geography: New Insights. Boulder, Colorado: Bureau of Audio-Visual Instruction, University of Colorado, 1969. (16 mm, sound, b/w)

Materials and activities of inquiry-oriented high school geography program.

8. Another useful procedure in preparing for inquiry teaching is to discuss inquiry teaching with specialists in order to clarify the strategy and its most useful techniques. Participating in a class (not observing some selected students) in a lesson or two designed to demonstrate inquiry teaching, followed by extensive analysis with the inquiry specialist (this is a must—real insights occur in the debriefing) will be most useful in developing an understanding of the nature and implications of inquiry teaching.

9. Reading, looking, and analyzing, however, are not sufficient preparation for successful inquiry teaching. It must be practiced too. One should begin by teaching lessons and using materials already designed for inquiry teaching. A number of these sample lessons are available from publishers and curriculum development projects, including:

High School Geography Project (available from Crowell Collier and Macmillan):

Unit II—Manufacturing and Agriculture (including the superb Game of Farming), 1969.

Unit III—Cultural Geography, 1969.

Unit VI—Japan, 1970. (This unit is one of the best model inquiry-teaching units in existence.)

Holt Social Studies Curriculum units (a set of three experimental units available from Holt, Rinehart & Winston):

A New History of the United States

Comparative Political Systems

The Shaping of Western Society

Teacher's Guide with lesson plans and visual masters for all three of the above units.

Anthropology Curriculum Study Project units (available from ACSP, 5632 Kimbark Avenue, Chicago, Ill. 60637). Each unit includes student learning materials (charts, maps, evidence cards, and reading materials) as well as teaching guides:

Study of Early Man

Great Transformation

Amherst Project units (available from Addison-Wesley Publishing Co.):

What Happened on Lexington Green? An Inquiry Into the Nature and Study of History

Korea and the Limits of Limited War

Ideally a teacher should make a video tape of himself as he teaches these lessons so that in replaying the lessons, he might analyze what went on in the students' heads and why each lesson was a success or failure. If this is not possible, perhaps he could ask several fellow teachers to observe his class and to discuss it with him afterward. Better yet, at the conclusion of the lesson he might ask the students in the class to describe their perceptions of what was going on and their reactions to it, of what he did and what they were doing or supposed to do. This type of feedback will be most useful in the next stage of preparation.

10. At this time you should try your own hand at designing some inquiry-teaching learning experiences—and then teach them. First, you should design some simple one, two, or three-day inquiry lessons involving content with which you are most familiar. These should be developed in cooperation with several other teachers, if possible, for several heads are immeasurably better than one in creating new teaching approaches. These lessons should then be analyzed by the group and revised until a workable plan emerges.

11. Finally, you must teach your own inquiry lessons, perhaps first to a group of your fellow teachers and then to your own class. Each effort should be examined critically by you, by your fellow teachers, and by the students. If several teachers can teach the same lesson and each can observe the others doing so, insights of even greater value may be developed. As a result, inquiry teaching, if and when finally undertaken as the primary instructional strategy in your classroom, will have every chance of meeting with success.

Careful preparation and practice are quite essential to successful and self-satisfying inquiry teaching. Because this type of strategy casts both student and teacher in new roles, it can be very frustrating and perhaps discouraging at first. How it is introduced to the students who are probably already accustomed to another teaching style will largely determine how it is accepted. If your students have never had to think for themselves, to ask questions and not get the answers, then inquiry teaching will be most difficult for them the first few weeks. If the teacher is inexperienced in inquiry teaching—has neither studied nor practiced it—he too may become quickly disillusioned. The change to inquiry teaching normally takes time. Knowing this may make the transition easier and may also prevent a premature abandonment of the strategy.

Perhaps a note sent to the author recently will best point up this type of situation. It was penned by a teacher who had just returned to his classroom after devoting a year to graduate study in geography and inquiry teaching:

> A pox on you and your (darn) inquiry method of teaching. I am working like a dog in an attempt to espouse your methods and am not really sure that the current results are worth the effort. I am considering going back to my old techniques of having three films and two reprimands each week. It saves on planning time.
>
> Seriously, I am getting some commendable results with some outstandingly "stupid" children. The only problem is finding the time to prepare for my lessons and making them come off the way they should. But it's getting better rapidly.

Inquiry teaching is difficult, especially at first. But it is by no means impossible. It can be precisely organized and executed. When mastered, it is fun and indeed worthwhile. No other teaching strategy may be used for as wide a range of objectives as inquiry teaching. This teaching strategy means teaching for conceptual objectives, using multimedia, involving students actively in the learning process, using data as a vehicle instead of merely an end in itself, and making the classroom an arena of thinking. It is by far the most exciting and challenging type of teaching available for use in social studies classrooms today. It requires extensive study and practice in order to use it successfully. This volume may be a start. The rest is up to you!

DATE DUE